A Child's WAR

GROWING UP ON THE HOME FRONT

MIKE BROWN

D0994785

Dedicated to my father, who
taught me to love history

First published in 2000
This edition published in 2010

The History Press
The Mill, Brimscombe Port
Stroud, Gloucestershire, GL5 2QG
www.thehistorypress.co.uk

British Library Cataloguing in Publication Data.
A catalogue record for this book is available from the British Library.

ISBN 978 0 7524 5858 8

Typesetting and origination by The History Press
Printed in Great Britain
Manufacturing managed by Jellyfish Print Solutions Ltd

Contents

Acknowledgements

I would like to take this opportunity to thank the following people who so kindly shared their memories with me: Mike Bree, Elizabeth Brown, Christine Castro (née Pilgrim), Eric Chisnall, Roy Coles, Margaret Cook (née Ladd), Michael Corrigan, Barbara Daltrey, Derek Dimond, June Edwards (née Fidler), Gwendolen Fox, David George, Charles Harris, Sylvie Harris (née Stevenson), Vivien Higgins (née Hatton), R.J. Holley, Ken Kessie, Barbara Ladd (née Courtney), Kitty Lawrence (née Pledger), Carol Mead (née Smith), John Merritt, Margery Neave, George Parks, D.J. Ryall, Geoff Shute, Iris Smith, Joyce Somerville, Margaret Woodrow. I am grateful to Lewisham Local Studies Centre for allowing me to reproduce extracts from Alan Miles's letters.

My thanks also go to the following who allowed me to use illustrations:

Photographs

Sylvie Harris (née Stevenson)
Kent Messenger Group Newspapers
Kitty Lawrence (née Pledger)
Lewisham Local Studies Centre
Ewa Lind
The Scout

Illustrations

Beano (D.C. Thompson & Co. Ltd)
British Red Cross
Express Newspaper Group Ltd
HMSO
Macmillans Ltd
Radio Times
RSPCA

Introduction

When the Second World War broke out in September 1939, it came as no surprise to the children of Germany; the Nazis had been preparing them for war through semi-military training in the Hitler Youth and the League of German Maidens, almost since they had taken control of the country back in 1933. To British children it was an altogether different matter – true, the situation in Europe had been looking threatening for some time, but British children then were no more interested in 'the news' than their descendants are today.

Everyone was affected by the war: men, women, and children. Although some people were far safer than others, no one could claim complete safety from the bombing raids or, later, the V1 flying bombs and the V2 rockets. On a more day-to-day level, everyone was affected by rationing, the black-out, shortages and the thousand and one small changes that the war brought with it.

This book seeks to look at those changes through the eyes of the children of the war, concentrating on those aspects of the home front that most concerned or interested them. It focuses on the war through eye-witness accounts by people who were children then, supported by photographs and artefacts. In addition there are activities from the period, such as recipes, things to make, and quizzes.

I hope the book will help those born after the war to understand what it was like for the children of the time, and bring back some fond memories to those who lived through it.

The Second World War did not just suddenly happen. In Germany Adolf Hitler and his National Socialist German Workers's Party (the Nazis) had been voted into power in 1933, and soon set about getting back the parts of Germany that had been taken away by the Treaty of Versailles (1919–20), which ended the First World War – or the Great War, as it was then called. At first people in Britain were not too worried; many said that the Germans had been badly treated following their defeat and were only taking back what belonged to them; some even said that Hitler was a strong and gifted leader and that we might do well to copy him.

In March 1936 Hitler took back the Rhineland. Four months later, when civil war broke out in Spain between supporters of the left-wing Republican government and the right-wing Nationalists in July 1936, he and his ally, Italy's dictator Benito Mussolini, sent 'volunteer' troops and aircraft to support the Nationalist forces. The war became a testing ground for modern weapons and methods of warfare, including air raids against towns and cities, the most famous of which was by German aircraft on the town of Guernica in April 1937. Cinema newsreel pictures of the bombing were seen by thousands in Britain – this was a time when most British families went to the cinema at least once a week.

Two years later, on 11 March 1938, German troops marched into Austria. But the real crunch came in September of that year. Hitler demanded a part of Czechoslovakia called the Sudetenland – this had never been German territory, so the argument that he just wanted to get back the former bits of Germany could not apply to it. The Czechoslovakian government refused to give in, so did Hitler; Europe seemed to be heading for another war – everyone's worst nightmare. The British Prime Minister, Neville Chamberlain, met with Hitler, the French Prime Minister and Mussolini in Munich on 29 September and the Sudetenland was handed over. Chamberlain returned saying that he had achieved 'Peace for our time', but few believed it. Hitler claimed that the Sudetenland was his 'last territorial demand' – even fewer believed that.

The 'Munich Crisis', as it was called, had taken Britain to the brink of war. Trenches were dug in the parks, the emergency services were put on full alert, and plans were drawn up to evacuate all London schoolchildren on the last day of the month. Although the evacuation plan was called off, 4,000 children from nurseries and special schools were taken away to the country, a foretaste of what was to come.

More and more, people felt that war was on the way, a war that Britain was not ready for – this was underlined when Hitler took over the rest of Czechoslovakia in March 1939. What Chamberlain had done was to buy time. In January 1939 the British Parliament had brought in the ARP (Air Raid Precautions) Act, which made local councils responsible for setting up safety measures such as the black-out, air-raid warnings and shelters to protect civilians. It also required them to get ARP services under way: air-raid wardens (to enforce the black-out), emergency casualty services and rescue squads. In March the Home Secretary made an appeal on the radio for one million ARP volunteers. Increasingly, throughout 1938 and into 1939, there were series of local ARP exercises where the new services put on public displays of fire-fighting and of dealing with air-raid 'victims'.

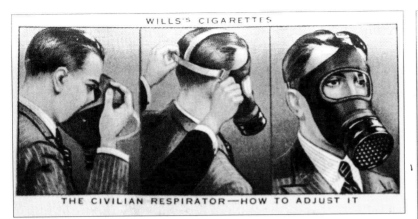

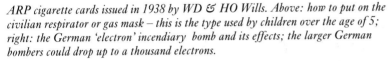

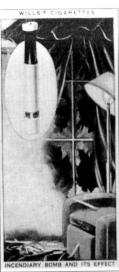

ARP cigarette cards issued in 1938 by WD & HO Wills. Above: how to put on the civilian respirator or gas mask – this is the type used by children over the age of 5; right: the German 'electron' incendiary bomb and its effects; the larger German bombers could drop up to a thousand electrons.

In the late 1930s, through these and other preparations going on around them, the children of Britain became aware of the threat of war. In the 1920s and 1930s, most brands of cigarette contained a picture card in every packet. Each card was part of a set, usually of fifty, with different titles: 'Film Stars', 'Cars', 'Aeroplanes', 'Footballers', and so on. One of the most popular pastimes among children, especially boys, was collecting and swapping cigarette cards, which they would cadge from grown-up relatives or neighbours. In 1938 a new set was issued. Called 'ARP', it was issued throughout 1938 and 1939 by five different brands, including Will's Woodbines, Churchman's and Ogden's, and would have been collected by many thousands of children. It contained cards showing different aspects of Air Raid Precautions, such as building a gas-proof 'refuge room' at home, or how to extinguish an incendiary bomb.

The preparations continued; in July 1939, every house in the country received four Civil Defence pamphlets explaining 'Some things you should know if war should come'. One of these pamphlets was on evacuation, especially that of children. Then, in August, London and large areas of the south-east were involved in a massive black-out practice.

During the summer of 1939 Hitler turned his attention to Poland. Britain and France had promised to support Poland, but Hitler believed that they would once again give way. When the British Ambassador warned that they were serious, Hitler replied that he was 50 years old and would prefer war now rather than when he was 55 or 60. At the end of August he began to make impossible demands on Poland. Without waiting for the Polish government's reply, the German army invaded Poland in the early hours of Friday 1 September 1939.

Britain and France declared war on 3 September. No one was prepared for war at this point and there followed a period of mobilisation, training and preparation by both sides and nothing much seemed to be happening – the so-called 'phoney war'.

On the home front the war seemed to be nothing more than a series of inconvenient restrictions such as the black-out. The introduction of rationing in January 1940 only served to strengthen this view. The newspapers headed calls for cut backs in the ARP and Auxiliary Fire Services, widely seen as 'army dodgers', and there was a steady drift-back of evacuees; almost 1 million had returned by the end of January.

In the first winter of the war enemy aircraft activity was confined to attacks on shipping in the English Channel, or mine laying around the coast. The first civilian air-raid death in Britain was during an attack on the Orkneys's naval base on 16 March 1940, and the first in England was not until the end of April, even then it was caused by a German mine-laying bomber crashing at Clacton-on-Sea, killing its crew as well as two civilians.

In May Germany began the Blitzkrieg; first German troops invaded Denmark, which fell in one day, then Norway, which fell in three weeks. On 10 May German armoured columns struck at Belgium, Holland, France and Luxembourg. Britain and France poured soldiers into Belgium to stem the flood of German troops – the same day that Neville Chamberlain resigned and Winston Churchill became Prime Minister.

On 14 May Holland surrendered, followed by Belgium on 17th. By 21 May German tanks had reached the Channel in France, splitting the Allied armies, and from 27 May to 3 June the Dunkirk evacuation took place – 225,000 British and 110,000 French and Belgian troops were plucked from the beaches by the fleet of 'little ships'. On 17 June Paris fell and on 21st the French government asked the Germans to make peace. Britain now stood alone.

Invasion was expected at any time, and a series of anti-invasion measures was brought in. In May 1940 the Home Guard was formed, beaches were mined, road blocks and tank traps sprang up everywhere, railway station name boards and road direction signs were removed. Everyone was on the look out for spies and fifth columnists. 'Careless Talk Costs Lives' the posters warned, car radios were banned, people taking photographs or making sketches were likely to be arrested. Invasion fever had reached a pitch by early September, as had the duel between the RAF and the Luftwaffe for control of the skies above Britain, otherwise known as the Battle of Britain.

On 7 September the Luftwaffe turned its attention to London. On that day, called 'Black Saturday' by the Londoners, the docks were pounded in the first of almost three months of nightly attacks on the capital. With the onset of autumn, the fear of invasion receded, to be replaced by the threat of aerial assault, and London was not the only target. The industrial towns and ports of Britain were also targets, and on 14 November Coventry was severely hit in a concentrated attack that paralysed the city. The year ended with the 'Second Great Fire of London' when the historic City of London was all but destroyed in a fire-bomb raid, which produced some of the war's most memorable pictures of St Paul's Cathedral ringed with fire and smoke.

The spring of 1941 re-awakened invasion fears, but in June Germany turned her attention to the east. The occupation of Russia also marked the end of the Big Blitz, as the massed raids of the previous nine months were called, although not the end of raiding, which continued in one form or another for the next two years. August saw the formation of the National Fire Service and the Fire Guard in response to the fire raids of the Big Blitz; millions of civilians not already involved in voluntary service in the Home Guard or ARP were ordered to attend compulsory training in incendiary bomb fighting, followed by stints of fire watching. In 1941 clothes rationing was introduced and the USA entered the war when Japan attacked Pearl Harbor in December.

In April 1942 the Baedeker raids on Britain's historic cathedral towns and cities began. Cities such as York, Norwich and Exeter, among others, were badly hit in a series of heavy raids that continued until July. At this point the 'tip and run' raids began, which as their name indicates were fast raids preceded by little or no warning, continuing until January 1944. In 1942 the first American troops began to arrive in Britain in the build up to the invasion of Europe.

In January 1944 there began the first of a series of intense incendiary bomb raids, known as 'the Little Blitz', and these continued until March of that year. In June 1944 came the Normandy landings and in the same month the first V1s landed in Britain, followed three months later by the first V2.

The Normandy landings were followed by a series of fiercely contested battles. Those who had predicted that it would soon be over were proved wrong as another wartime Christmas came, although by then the end was clearly in sight.

A family learning how to fit and use their gas masks.

By the end of the year the threat of a German invasion was gone; the Home Guard was stood-down on 1 November.

Attacks by German aircraft on Britain had ceased and the numbers of civil defence workers were cut back, except in the south-east, where V weapons continued to fall. The last V2 landed in Orpington, Kent, on Wednesday 27 March 1945, and one woman was killed, becoming the last civilian death of the war, and twenty-three were seriously injured. The last V1s were launched on the evening of 28/29 March. Most were shot down, but one landed at Waltham Abbey, one at Chislehurst. The very last doodlebug touched down somewhat fittingly, in a sewage farm at Datchworth, near Hatfield. The Civil Defence were wound up on 2 May and held a final parade on 10 June in Hyde Park, where they were reviewed by the King. On 2 May the newspapers announced the death of Hitler, and four days later Germany surrendered unconditionally, the following day being declared VE Day.

Japan fought on, but the dropping of two atomic bombs in August resulted in their surrender, and VJ Day. The war was finally completely over.

ONE

The Day the War Broke Out[*]

I was 13 when the war started. The week before it broke out my family – me, Mum and Dad, and my little sister Eileen – went to Weymouth on holiday. We went to the cinema to see Fred Astaire and Ginger Rogers and on the newsreel they were saying that war was coming. We came home on Friday instead of Saturday – the train was packed – there were sixteen in our compartment instead of eight.

Iris Smith, Bristol

On the morning of Sunday 3 September 1939 it was announced that the Prime Minister would make a radio broadcast to the nation at 11.15 am. Everyone held their breath; would Neville Chamberlain once again manage to turn certain war into peace at the last moment, as he had done at Munich the year before?

At the announced time the Prime Minister spoke:

This morning, the British Ambassador in Berlin handed the German Government a final note stating that unless we heard from them by eleven o'clock that they were prepared at once to withdraw their troops from Poland a state of war would exist between us.

I have to tell you now that no such undertaking has been received, and that consequently this country is at war with Germany.

The Second World War had begun. Roy Coles, also from Bristol, recalls listening to the broadcast: 'I was eleven when the war started. That Sunday morning I listened to the radio with my Dad, we listened in silence as war was declared. We had to go and see my Grandmother and my Great Aunt, we walked in silence down to my Gran's – there was virtually nobody about. My Gran didn't have a radio so we told them.'

* Catchphrase of the contemporary comedian Rob Wilton.

Mothers being shown how to use the baby gas helmet. (Kent Messenger Newspaper Group)

The news rapidly filtered through to those who, like Roy's gran, did not hear the broadcast; Vivien Hatton from Bermondsey remembers: 'We were in church when the vicar told us that we were at war.' Almost immediately after Chamberlain's broadcast, an air-raid warning (a false alarm as it turned out) was sounded in London and large parts of south-east England. Sylvie Stevenson from Chingford was 4 at the time: 'The first I knew was when the air-raid sirens went, we were at the top of Hall Lane – everyone just stopped. I remember dad coming home that evening, saying he was going to join up – Mum went berserk.' Charles Harris, also from Chingford, was aged 7; he too remembers that first air-raid warning: 'When the sirens went I went down into the public shelter, it was dark inside – there were no lights. Down in the mud on the floor I found 6*d*, when I came out I bought three tubs of ice cream with it – they were 2*d* each – my brother and sister and me all had ice cream that afternoon.'

Although some of the changes that the war brought to the lives of children did not come about immediately (rationing, for example, only came in later, as the war dragged on), others had already been introduced before the outbreak of war, such as gas masks, or followed almost immediately, as with ID cards and the spread of Anderson shelters.

TWO

Evacuation

As the threat of war had increased during in the late 1930s, the government had begun laying plans for evacuation. These directly affected children, especially those living in London, the industrial cities and the great ports.

There had been air raids on Britain in the First World War and people were very concerned about the danger they posed. In the summer of 1938, it was decided that, should war come, those least able to fend for themselves – children, the elderly and the disabled – should be evacuated from those places most under threat. In September, at the time of the Munich crisis, plans were drawn up splitting the country into three types of area: Evacuation; Neutral; and Reception. Evacuation areas were mainly those places where people were thought to be in the most danger of air attack, although some places were cleared of civilians to provide training areas for the forces. The first Evacuation areas included Greater London, the Medway towns, Merseyside, Portsmouth, Birmingham, Manchester, Sheffield, Leeds, Newcastle, Edinburgh and Glasgow. Reception areas were safer parts to which evacuees – those being evacuated – would be taken; they were mainly rural areas such as Kent, East Anglia and Wales.

Schools were to be evacuated *en masse*, the children and their teachers moving all together to the same area, where they would usually share the neighbourhood school with the local children. Children from the same family would go together, with the younger ones going with the eldest's school. Pre-school children were to be evacuated with their mothers.

On Monday 28 August 1939, before the summer holidays had actually ended, London schoolchildren went back to school to take part in an evacuation rehearsal. Many of the children had assembled by 6 am, carrying their kit. A government leaflet outlined what this should comprise: 'a handbag or case containing the child's gas mask, a change of under-clothing, night clothes, house shoes or plimsolls, spare stockings or socks, a toothbrush, a comb, towel, soap and face cloth, handkerchiefs; and, if possible, a warm coat or macintosh. Each child should bring a packet of food for the day.' Every school had been given a number and had been told when to go to which railway station or where to board the coaches. The cost of the journey was paid for by the government.

On the morning of 31 August 1939, three days before war broke out, the order was given for the evacuation plans to be put into operation, and during the next four days nearly 1.9 million people were evacuated, including almost 1.5 million children, over half of whom were in school parties. Parents of schoolchildren were told when their children's school would be leaving, although they did not learn the destination until after the children had got there; mothers of younger children were told where and when to assemble. From the London area alone 376,652 children and their teachers, 275,895 pre-school children and their mothers, 3,577 expectant mothers and 3,403 blind adults were transported out of the capital. Any operation involving these vast numbers could easily have lapsed into complete confusion but overall this phase of the operation was surprisingly successful.

Vivien Hatton was evacuated from Bermondsey

I was 9 years old when the war broke out, A few days beforehand I had been evacuated along with my older sister Audrey with her school, Aylwyn High School, to Worthing. I was terribly frightened. My mother made us sandwiches for the journey. We carried our gas masks round our necks and had a badge pinned to us to say who we were. We were billeted with a family I didn't like,

Evacuation of Caldecott Road School to Kent. Each London County Council school had a number, in this case 1103. Notice the LCC 1103 armband being worn by the male teacher, left. (Kent Messenger Newspaper Group)

they were quite dirty – we arrived there about nine o'clock but were given no food, so we lay in bed and finished our sandwiches. I cried but my sister told me not to be such a baby.

We had some friends who were billeted with a Salvation Army couple, Mr and Mrs Crump, and they said they could arrange for us to transfer to them. The Billeting Officer said we were very ungrateful children.

On the children's arrival at their destinations, the first real problems began to appear. It had not always been possible to transport schools to places where suitable, or even sufficient, school accommodation was available. The teachers set about putting things in order. Soon village halls and large buildings of all sorts had been put to use as temporary schoolrooms, and by Christmas almost all the evacuated children were receiving full-time education. At the beginning of the war Alan Miles, who was 9 at the time, was evacuated from New Cross to Brighton. His mother kept the letters he sent home, and they make a fascinating record. This is his first letter (spelling mistakes and all):

"MR. CHAMB'LAIN'S SENT ME TO ASK IF YOU C'N TAKE IN ANY 'VACUEES," SAID WILLIAM.

'William' illustration from William and the Evacuees, *published 1940. (Macmillan Publishers)*

Dear Mum,

I am having a nice time. I went to school on Monday and in the prak [park] in the Afternoon. Do you know that I have tow [two] shillings and nine pence and I buot [bought] two commics one is Larks and the other is tip Top. I hop Tinker [his cat] is all right and reads this letter out which I am just going to write miow miow miow for the cat. Is dady making some more guns and I hop dady's foot is better. Is mumy still finding the cat on my bed. Mrs bodmin went to the pictures and Enid and I went to fech Mrs bodmin and Mr bodmin.

Love from Alan

Another letter dated 2 July 1941 shows how contact with home was ensured – 'I am at school writing this letter as every Wensday morning Londers [Londoners] have to write letters home.'

One particular problem sprang up in North Wales, where some children were placed with Welsh-speaking families, but with the ready adaptability of youth, many soon picked up enough Welsh to get by, and their schools arranged for Welsh to be included in their lessons.

The months that followed soon came to be known as the 'phoney war'. Hitler had not expected Britain and France to go to war at this time and was not ready for a full-scale attack on them. Throughout the winter of 1939/40 the German U-boat assault on merchant shipping was pressed ahead, but on land and in the air almost nothing happened. The expected air raids failed to materialise and in Britain more civilians died in black-out traffic accidents than soldiers were killed by enemy action. Many evacuees were homesick, some had been hurriedly placed in the most unsuitable billets, dirty and insanitary, or with people unwilling or unable to look after them properly. Barbara Courtney from Nunhead remembers: 'We were evacuated to Salisbury, you always tried to be nice, tried to please. The woman where my brother and I were billeted, she said she'd burnt the rice pudding. I said I didn't mind, then I saw it – it was black. She cut all the bits off and put them on my plate. Her husband said, "You can't make her eat that!", but she said I'd said I liked it, so she made me.'

Many parents missed their children dreadfully, and as the precautions seemed to prove unnecessary, more and more evacuees came home – after only a few weeks the Minister of Health was advising mothers of young evacuees not

Under-5s being evacuated to war nurseries in the country by the WVS (Women's Voluntary Services). The woman on the right is in WVS uniform.

to bring them back to the cities, but by Christmas nearly half of all evacuees had returned.

Alan Miles wrote home on 26 January 1940: 'Mrs Gatehouse said to me that I am being moved but I do not want to move I want to come home. If you want to know why it is because I am getting a bit tired of being down here by my self and another thing is because I want to see my dear little Tinker. I think my teacher Mrs Howard has gone back and all my friends have gone back like Lawrence has gone back so that it is not very nice not to have friends.'

Sylvie Stevenson from Chingford, aged 4 when the war began, remembers:

I was evacuated for about two weeks, somewhere near Bedford. I'd never had cream before, and the lady said; 'Would you like some cream?' I said 'Yes', so she gave me kippers with cream! I hated being away from home and Mum and Dad came down and got me. Dad was in a reserved occupation, making ammunition boxes for the army.

We had a boy called Bernard Muggeridge at school, he didn't turn up for a long time – someone said he'd been killed in an air raid, someone else said he'd drunk the school ink and died. Later he came back – he'd been evacuated.

Then came the German invasion of western Europe, the 'Blitzkrieg'. With the fall of France in June 1940, Britain became the next target. Invasion was expected on the south coast of England, which was hastily changed from a Reception area to an Evacuation area. Hurriedly over 200,000 children in the area were evacuated, or, in some cases, re-evacuated to Wales or the Midlands. Some were sent to America, but this was stopped when in September the *City of Benares*, a ship carrying evacuees there, was torpedoed and sunk. Apart from this, evacuees were relatively safe; in the first two years of bombing, the heaviest part of the Blitz, only twenty-seven evacuees were killed by enemy action.

On the whole, most of the evacuees who were part of the official government scheme came from the poorer and more crowded parts of the big cities. The children of the urban middle and upper classes often went to live with relatives or schoolfriends in the country. Vivien Hatton recalls: 'The school asked the girls who lived in the North of England if they would take one of us to stay for the summer holidays; I went up to Birmingham with one girl – I hated it. I wrote to my mother saying "Please, please, can I come home?" She wrote back saying that there was only the kitchen and shelter left to come back to – we'd been blasted!'

Ministry of Health poster underlining the message that children should be evacuated from London. Posters were everywhere during the war giving all sorts of messages. (HMSO)

Babies and toddlers being evacuated at Maidstone. (Kent Messenger Newspaper Group)

The countryside to which the official evacuees had been moved seemed a different world from that of the inner-city tenements and slums many of them had come from, but on the whole they soon adjusted. The streets were exchanged for the fields, city dogs and cats for cows and sheep, packaged food for farm goods. With the open air and fresh food many flourished. Alan Miles (July 1940): 'Every night when I come home from school I get the eggs for Mrs Colwill. Mr Colwill is letting me milk the cow tonight. There is another thing I do at night that is getting the cows and driving them home half a mile.'

Parents were expected to pay towards the keep of their evacuated children; in London this was set at 6s (30p) a week each, although poorer parents were charged less. People taking in evacuees were paid more, from 8s 6d (43p) up to 16s 6d (83p), depending on the age of the children, the difference being made up by the state.

Evacuation was not just a one-way process. In June 1940, 29,000 civilians were evacuated to mainland Britain from the Channel Islands, and in September 1940

Evacuees arriving in Kent. (Kent Messenger Newspaper Group)

Children playing in a WVS war nursery. The woman on the right is Lady Reading, the leader of the WVS, in WVS uniform.

about 2,000 children from Gibraltar were evacuated from there to London. Few spoke any English, but they soon settled in, with several Scout groups being set up for them. They eventually returned to Gibraltar in the summer of 1944. And they were by no means unique; refugees from all over Europe had come to Britain seeking safety, starting with German Jews in the early 1930s, among them many children.

At about the same time as the Allies landed in Normandy in June 1944, a new air assault began, first from the V1s, the 'doodlebugs', then from the V2 rockets. A new wave of evacuation took place between July and September, although before it could even begin more than 200 under-16s had been killed. In the first two weeks 170,000 official evacuees left, along with half a million who made their own way out of the target areas, but again many soon returned as the threat proved less serious than expected.

THREE

Children in the Front Line

Children who had stayed in the cities, or whose parents had taken them home again after they had been evacuated, were to find themselves with ringside seats when the air raids began. But in the first winter of the war, 1939–40, enemy aircraft activity was confined to attacks on shipping in the English Channel, or mine-laying around the coast. The first civilian air-raid death in Britain was during an attack on the Orkneys's naval base on 16 March 1940, and the first in England was not until the end of April; even then it was caused by a German mine-laying bomber crashing at Clacton-on-Sea, killing its crew as well as two civilians. In the two years before the outbreak of war a series of measures had been introduced to counter, or at least minimise, the threat posed by bombing. These soon became part of everyday life.

AIR-RAID WARNINGS

In May 1938 the government had set out a system of air-raid warnings which would be sounded to warn of an imminent air attack, giving the public time to take cover. The warning would consist of a two-minute signal from a siren, rising and falling in pitch; the 'All-clear' signal would be given in the same way, but at a constant pitch. The up-and-down noise of the warning siren led to its becoming known as 'Wailing Willy' or 'Moaning Minnie'. The 'Alert' sound itself became hated – some people found it more frightening than the noise of the actual raids. But most felt like Christine Pilgrim of Peckham: 'When you heard the siren, it wasn't so much that it frightened you – you knew what you had to do – it was, "Oh no, not again!" '

The siren was followed by a second type of warning, which indicated what kind of bomb was being dropped. For poison gas the air-raid wardens sounded a gas rattle (a kind of huge, old-fashioned football rattle), to warn people to put on their gas masks. The gas 'All-clear' was given by the ringing of hand-bells. If incendiary bombs were dropped, wardens or police sounded a series of short blasts on whistles, or, in some areas, banged dustbin lids, like gongs. This signalled that people should come out of their shelters and put out the fires. In *The City That Wouldn't Die*, Richard Collier describes one such occurrence: 'at Kennington, Station Officer Walter Bunday stopped short for a strange sight: a deserted street . . . a shower of incendiaries . . . every front door opening as one, and householders, silent and purposeful, whisking out to deal with them . . . men, women, small children, armed with sand and 'buckets of water. Then every front door shutting again like clockwork and not a word exchanged – "Like something out of Disney".'

There were several tests of the warning system in the months before war broke out, so that everyone recognised the sound immediately. From 1 September 1939 the sounding of sirens, or of factory hooters, which were used to back them up, was made illegal for any reason except for air-raid warnings.

SHELTERS

In just about every cowboy film ever made, there is a point in the shoot-out when somebody suddenly stands up, and is just as suddenly shot – it's pretty obvious that the rule is 'Get down and stay down'. A similar rule applies to being bombed: 'Take cover'. At first simple measures were used to provide cover, such as digging trenches, or the use of sandbags to make defensive walls, but these were clearly suitable only as stop-gap measures. Christine Pilgrim remembers: 'Dad putting bunks up in the cellar so that we could go down there in a raid.'

At the beginning of 1939, the government had announced the introduction of a small air-raid shelter which could be put up in the back garden of a house. The 'sectional steel shelter', as it was officially known, soon became universally called the 'Anderson' after the then Home Secretary, and was supplied free of charge to the poorer inhabitants of danger areas, and for a small fee to anyone else. It was delivered in sections and had to be put up by the householder. This entailed digging a large hole, in which the shelter was half buried, and the leftover earth was then piled on top to give added protection. Barbara Courtney remembers the arrival of an Anderson at her family's home in Nunhead: 'I was almost 5 when the war broke out. The first I knew about it was when they delivered our Anderson shelter. They delivered it in sections and you had to put it up. I helped my dad, well, I did a bit of digging – he did it really.'

Being half buried certainly added to the safety of the Anderson, but it also caused its chief problem; during wet weather it tended to fill up with water.

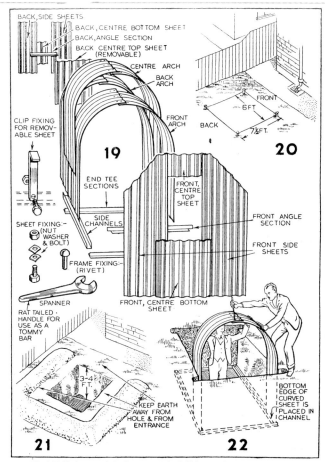

19. The individual parts of the Government Steel Shelter as they are delivered, with details of each part. 20. The actual site chosen should first be marked out in this manner. 21. This diagram shows the hole dug to its final depth. 22. Erecting the steel arches. Two men are required for this part of the task.

Putting up the 'Government Steel Shelter', better known as the Anderson shelter. From Modern Make and Mend, *published in 1939.*

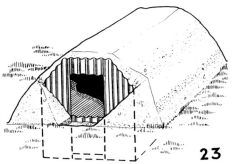

23. The Government Steel Shelter actually in position and provided with an earth capping. The steel parts of which the shelter is constructed will support 3 feet of soil all over, and it is recommended that a minimum of 15 inches of soil be provided.

Still, damp and uncomfortable as they were, although no shelter could survive a direct hit, there is no doubt that they saved many lives. Charles Harris from Chingford, then aged 7, remembers: 'There were three land mines came down near us, one went off in the reservoir, one failed to go off, and the third one caught in some telegraph wires and came down on a shelter about 100 yards down our road. They were all killed. We were in our shelter and the door came in and I got hit over the head. Three houses and two bungalows were wrecked, and all the rest had their windows blown out.' By mid-1940 over 2.25 million Andersons had been supplied.

However, many people did not have back gardens; for them the government produced a booklet, 'Your home as an air-raid shelter', which showed various ways of using mattresses, old doors, etc., to strengthen one of the downstairs rooms as a refuge. Other common practices were to use the cupboard under the stairs or to get under a table, but neither of these was completely satisfactory. Barbara Daltry from Windsor remembers one incident when she was 16: 'Once I was walking home in the black-out, it was 3 miles, when I got there Mother said, "Get under the table, there's an unexploded bomb in the back garden!" I told her I was too tired – if I was going to die, I'd die in bed. Actually the bomb was in the woods some way away.'

At the end of 1940, the government introduced a shelter for indoor use. Nicknamed the 'Morrison' after Herbert Morrison, the Minister of Home Defence, it was a low, steel cage, which, when not in use, could double up as a table.

Like the Anderson, the Morrison was delivered in sections and had to be assembled. A shortage of council workmen meant that people were encouraged to put up their own shelters, but this was often not possible, so youth groups such as the Scouts were brought in to help. Michael Corrigan was a Scout in Bristol:

Later during the war when we had air raids over Bristol many houses were issued with Morrison shelters which were solid metal, table-like constructions which were erected in the home, usually in the dining room, often taking the place of the dining table. The shelters were delivered in pieces and we were informed by the authorities of the addresses and we would then go out, after school, and erect them. This meant finding a suitable place in the house, moving any existing furniture out of the way, getting the solid metal legs in place and placing a very heavy solid sheet of metal on top and bolting the whole thing together. Interlaced metal strips were then stretched across the bottom

How to Use the Shelter as a Table

FIGURE 8

Illustrations from the booklet 'How to Put up Your Morrison Shelter', issued by the Ministry of Home Security in 1941.

framework ready for the householder to bring down their mattress and make it their bed as well as their shelter.

Obviously, people had to go out – work, shops, school, church and so on – and could not always be near home when the air-raid warning sounded. For this reason a number of public shelters were set up. These might be converted basements in shops, cinemas, etc., or specially built shelters. They were usually marked with a large 'S' in white on a black background, or vice versa, and there would be similar signs, painted on walls or hung from lamp-posts, which showed the way to the nearest shelter. Failing this, when the warning sounded, the local air-raid warden would grab any strangers and push them into the nearest public shelter, or, if there wasn't one, into the nearest private shelter where there was room. David George recalls the public shelters in Ealing: 'There were two big surface shelters built in our street. We spent many nights in them. The wardens woke us up and we used to go down for the whole night.'

The councils made use of whatever local facilities existed; in places like Dover and Chislehurst, the caves were used – bunks were set up, as well as first-aid posts,

Children being taught in the Elephant & Castle Underground station during a raid. They are sitting on the special tube station three-tiered bunks, the middle one of which swung down to form a seat.

toilets, and other facilities. In London, after first refusing to allow it, the government agreed that the Underground stations be used as shelters; at the height of the Blitz over 140,000 people were sleeping in the stations – so many that special three-tier bunks were put up, and 'tube refreshment' trains were laid on, selling tea, cakes, etc. But in the early months of the war, precautions were still makeshift.

GAS MASKS

One of the weapons introduced in the First World War had been poison gas. As far back as 1935 the government had decided to build up stocks of gas masks to be given free to all members of the public, so that at the time of the Munich crisis many civilians were issued with one. During the summer of 1939 almost everyone else received theirs, except for babies and small children, who needed special masks; these were mostly issued later that year. Posters encouraged people to take their gas masks with them wherever they went – one of the first problems created by gas masks was that vast numbers of them were absent-mindedly left on buses, trains and the Underground.

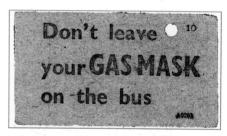

The gas mask developed for babies was actually called a gas hood, or protective helmet (it was generally known as the baby-bag). It was designed for children up to the age of about 18 months and an official leaflet, produced in July 1939, described it as follows:

Message printed on the back of a bus ticket: so many gas masks were left on London Transport in the first few weeks of the war that a special lost property office for gas masks was set up.

> The helmet consists of a hood, made of impervious fabric and fitted with a large window, which encloses the head, shoulders and arms, and is closed around the waist by means of a draw tape. A baby when it is in is thus able to get its hand to its mouth. The hood is surrounded by and fastened to a light metal frame, which is lengthened on the underside and fitted with an adjustable tail-piece, so as to form a support and protection to a baby's back. . . . The metal frame and supporting strap may be varied in length to suit all sizes of babies and children up to about five years of age.

The reason for this higher age of 5 was so that it could be used for children 'temperamentally unsuited for wearing a respirator'.

Last to be produced was a mask for young children below the age of 4–5 years; officially called the 'Small Child's respirator', it was commonly called the Mickey Mouse mask. Similar in style to the adult mask, it was produced in bright red and blue, to try to make the toddlers more keen to wear it. The official leaflet pointed out that it fastened with a hook-and-eye fitting at the back, to make it more difficult for a small child to take it off. One book, published in 1942, advised parents on how to encourage their younger children to wear their gas masks:

Particularly children under six should be accustomed to wearing their gas masks through play. If you wait until there is an emergency it is going to be very difficult indeed to get them to wear them for any length of time. If you make it a game they will be much more inclined to lose all fear of the mask and they will be willing to wear them for longer and longer periods. Whenever you get a child to wear his mask, be sure to wear yours at the same time. That will make it imitative play and they will feel they are being 'grown up' in wearing one. I should not use the words 'poison gas' in explaining to the child the purpose of the mask, but say that one day the Germans might try to use 'nasty smells that make us feel ill' and that we can avoid these by use of our gas masks. Also they should be taught to carry them from an early age, and for this we must set them a good example.

And that was not all; the sight of Mum or Dad in their gas mask was enough to send some smaller children into floods of terrified tears. The BBC broadcast the following advice: 'Are your little ones used to seeing you in your mask? Make a game of it, calling it "Mummy's funny face" or something of that kind.'

All masks were issued in a cardboard container, which could also be used, with the addition of a string handle, as a carrier. However, the boxes neither looked good nor wore well. Children typically found a thousand and one uses for them, such as goalposts, wickets in cricket, etc. Although the masks were issued free, you could be fined up to £5 if your mask was damaged or lost due to negligence, so many parents bought hard-wearing metal containers for their children's masks.

When the feared poison gas raids failed to materialise, people began increasingly to leave their gas masks at home as David George from South Ealing recalls: 'I was born in June 1939, so my memories are only of the last years of the war. I don't remember gas masks at all, I don't think anybody used them by then.'

Gas drill: notice the woman on the right's cloth gas-mask bag, the toddlers's gas masks and cardboard cases. (Kent Messenger Newspaper Group)

ID CARDS

On 1 September 1939, before war broke out, the National Registration Act was passed in Parliament, requiring all citizens of the country to register their details: name, address, age, etc. Registration duly took place on Friday 29 September 1939, when the war had begun, and over the next few days every person in Britain was issued with an identity card, green for adults and brown for children under 16 (cards were issued within a few weeks of a baby's birth). This was partly due to fears of German spies and parachutists; ID cards had to be shown at checkpoints set up by policemen, Home Guards or the armed services. But the information was also later used to issue ration cards, and the ID card had to be produced and stamped in order to obtain a new ration book when the old one ran out. This made it valuable, and forgeries and thefts were common – this report in the *Kentish Mercury* of March 1942 gives one example:

YOUTH WITH THREE IDENTITY CARDS
Leonard Eldridge (17) . . . was charged at Woolwich . . . with being in unlawful possession of an identity card. Det. Sergt. Davis said [he] gave a name other

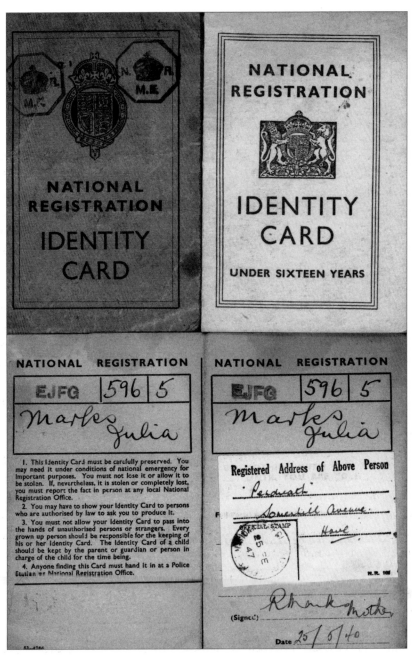

Children's buff-coloured identity cards – adults's cards were green. Upper left, early type issued from September 1939. Upper right, later type issued from 1943. Below, inside of early card; note that it is signed by the girl's mother, and that she changed address in 1947 (the inserted slip – right). Identity cards continued in use for some time after the war.

than Eldridge, and produced an identity card in that name. Two other cards were found on Eldridge in the same name, and the youth said he had picked them up at 'the Salvation Army place'. The Sergeant added that when they were alone Eldridge offered him £1 to let him go.

THE BLACK-OUT

At night cities can be seen from miles away by aircraft, due to the lighted buildings, street-lights, vehicle headlights, etc. In 1935 the government decided that, in the event of a war, lighting restrictions – or the black-out, as it soon came to be called – would be brought in to make life more difficult for enemy bombers.

In 1938 plans for the black-out were made public. Houses had to mask doors and windows so that no light was visible from the outside; this was usually done by the use of heavy black-out curtains. Street-lights and shop lights had to be turned off. Cars, lorries, and even bicycles had to have special headlight covers. An extract from an evacuee's letter home said: 'I hope you can get rear lights for bicycles in London. I could not send any money for it as the front light cost me 3/8d and 6d for a black-out for it'. Even a pocket torch had to give out only a small amount of light; this could be achieved by wrapping tissue paper over the front. A house showing a light would soon be visited by the police or air-raid wardens – 'Put that light out!' was one of the more famous cries of the Second World War – and repeated offences would land the culprit in court.

The black-out measures were very successful, but they had unexpected drawbacks; in November 1939 road deaths were up over 50 per cent on the previous November, even though over half a million cars had been taken off the road because of a severe rationing of petrol. And there were other dangers, as Charles Harris from Chingford remembers: 'We used to go to the youth club in the evening. I was running there one night in the black-out and ran straight into another boy running the other way. He was shorter than me and his head hit me right between the eyes. Next day my eyes were closed right up.' To try to improve matters the government urged people to wear something white at night, white lines were painted down the middle of roads for the first time, and white stripes were painted around roadside trees, street-lights, pillar-boxes, etc.

On 10 May Germany launched the Blitzkrieg. On 21 June France sued for peace – in a mere six weeks Germany had over-run the whole of western Europe except Britain. But Britain expected an immediate German invasion. The Local Defence Volunteers had been formed a month earlier, on 14 May; soon to be renamed

ONE LUCAS "MASKLITE"

A.R.P. Cycle Headlamp Shield

(Fully Patented and Registered)

* Immediately converts your Headlamp to exact requirements of War-Time Lighting Restrictions. *(See back of envelope.)*

* No Painting. No Blacking and spoiling of Reflector.

* Your Lamp looks a clean neat job with this shield, not a makeshift.

* Fitted in a few seconds to Lucas or other Lamps.

PRICE 6d.

JOSEPH LUCAS LTD., BIRMINGHAM, 19.

Extract from OFFICIAL WAR-TIME LIGHTING RESTRICTIONS *relating to* CYCLE LAMPS :—
"The upper half of the front glass must be completely obscured ; the lower half of any reflector must be treated with black paint or otherwise rendered non-effective."

PLEASE RETAIN THIS PACKET FOR POLICE INSPECTION IF NECESSARY.

SHIELD IN OPERATION

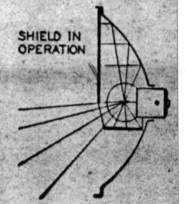

Packet containing Lucas 'Masklite' ARP bicycle headlamp black-out shield.

the Home Guard, or, more commonly, 'Dad's Army'. They were a volunteer force made up of men too old or lads too young for the services – at first the minimum age for joining was 15, later raised to 16. What the Home Guard lacked in expertise was often made up for in enthusiasm; as a Boy Scout, Michael Corrigan was involved in Home Guard and ARP exercises in Bristol:

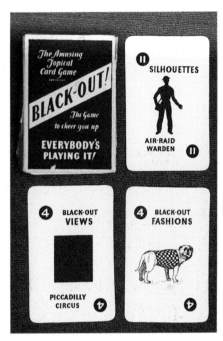

Black-out playing cards – 'Everybody's playing it'; games like this were popular at the beginning of the war – it was all a bit of fun then, but later things got more serious and such games lost favour.

> During one exercise, in which the local Home Guard were involved, the only tank in Bristol was supposed to be the enemy and the Home Guard were to defend one of the roads into the city and pretend to stop it. Well, the local Home Guard knew how to stop tanks, you put a large piece of wood between the tracks and the sprocket wheels, and the tracks snap. In their enthusiasm the Home Guards actually put this knowledge into practice and disabled the only tank which we had to defend Bristol. As you can imagine, with all this going on we 'casualties' were soon told to get off home before black-out.

Britain prepared for invasion: signposts at crossroads and corners, railway station name-boards, etc., anything that could help the enemy know where they were, were hastily removed. Mike Bree from Penzance remembers:

> As well as perfectly ridiculous suggestions such as handing in any maps we had of Britain, any postcards or the like which might aid the enemy, and removing all road signs, station names, even the town names from pub landlords' licensing boards, etc., we were told not to keep any personal diaries or records. It was suggested that any cameras or films be handed over to be used by HM forces. This was no joke for, in no time at all, it was almost a case of being arrested as a spy should one be seen anywhere strategic with a camera, which could result in its confiscation; also, it was impossible, very soon, to get films for cameras.

Sylvie Stevenson: 'You never saw a motorbike. One day I saw a man on his motorbike with a leather hat and coat on – I ran home as fast as I could – I thought the Germans had invaded.'

Leaflets were distributed telling people what to do in the event of an invasion. Road-blocks were set up, concrete gun emplacements called pill-boxes were built at crossroads and in other important positions, and along the south and east coasts where the invasion was expected the beaches were planted with mines and defended by barbed wire and more pill-boxes.

Carol Smith from Dunstable recalls: 'As a teenager in wartime I had a reasonable time. The most annoying restriction was not being able to go to the coast because of bunkers and barbed wire on the beaches. However, we had the Girl Guides and the Girls's Club.'

During July and August German air attacks on Britain focused on the south and east during the day, and the manufacturing towns at night, but London was left alone. The next step came in August: because the German army could not invade while the RAF and the Royal Navy could sink their ships and troop transports in the Channel, the RAF had to be destroyed.

Herman Goering, chief of the Luftwaffe, flung his planes into an all-out assault on the RAF, attacking the airfields, command posts and radar stations. This became the crucial period in what Churchill called 'the Battle of Britain'. Heavily outnumbered, the fighter pilots of the RAF went up time and time again to take on the Luftwaffe's massed attacks. All over the south of England people watched the dog-fights going on overhead. George Parks of Deptford vividly remembers them: 'We used to stand and watch the dog-fights, way up in the air – vapour trails weaving in and out. Then one of them would come down in flames – we'd all cheer like mad – of course we didn't know who it was, but we were sure it must be a German!' But of course they weren't all Germans – John Merritt of Virginia Water, Surrey: 'A vivid memory of those early war years concerns a Hawker Hurricane fighter that flew over the school one playtime. Suddenly, and to our horror, the whole tailplane fell off and the Hurricane spiralled down and crashed into the local gravel and sand pit. The pilot was later found dead, still in the cockpit. Of course that sand pit became famous as the Thorpe Park Leisure Centre.'

Then the target changed: the bombers turned north towards London. At teatime on Saturday 7 September 1940 the Observer Corps (whose job it was to keep track of enemy aircraft) watched a large force of over 300 German bombers as it flew north over Kent to the Thames estuary, turning westward to follow the river into London. In the late Saturday afternoon, Londoners watched as the planes flew steadily on; then, over the dock areas of the East End, they began to drop their bombs. Smoke billowed as one warehouse after another was hit and caught fire; then, as night drew on, other waves of bombers came, using the fires started by the first wave as a target. And what a target – the flames could be seen for miles, warehouses full of spirits, sugar, wood, and other inflammable goods blazed. Barbara Daltrey lived in Windsor: 'I remember when they bombed the London Docks, we were 25 miles away but the whole sky was lit up with a red glow.'

Sylvie Stevenson from Chingford saw the devastation at close quarters: 'My grandfather was a fire-watcher at Lyon's Corner House in Piccadilly. The morning after the first big raid on London he didn't come home, so Mum took me on a bus down there. He was all right, and I remember he took me up on the roof, it was unbelievable – over to the east there was smoke and rubble everywhere and buildings were still on fire.'

Derek Dimond lived in Tottenham: 'I remember going up to Liverpool Street from Stanstead with my Dad. I was deeply struck by the bomb damage – smoke and ruins everywhere.'

That night 430 civilians were killed and 1,600 injured. The next evening the Luftwaffe came again, and the next. The RAF fought back – the Battle of Britain reached its peak in mid-September. London was to be raided almost every night from 7 September to early November. But it is all too easy to think that London was the only target – on 14 November, instead of hitting London, the bombers flew on into the Midlands; this time the target was Coventry. The destruction was appalling; one third of all the houses in the town were destroyed, and the Germans started to use a new word, to 'coventrate': it meant the destroying of a city.

Carol Smith saw, and heard, the planes going over Dunstable: 'The night Coventry was bombed planes came over our house in droves, it was a continuous drone – we could see the sky lit up like a bonfire, it was like it was just down the road. Next day we couldn't believe it was as far away as Coventry, all of 70 miles.'

Eric Chisnall witnessed the after-effects, when he visited the city with a party of Scouts:

I shall never forget seeing the state of Coventry Cathedral after the German bombers had done their worst. On small pieces of walls that were still standing we could see where the lead guttering, hoppers, and downpipes, had melted and run down the walls, piles of rubble were everywhere, and yet the main tower was still standing. We were able to climb the stone spiral staircase to the top and look over the scene of devastation. I remember feeling quite dizzy when I reached the ground again – could this have been because we had a bit of a race down the steps? Another memory of Coventry was having our mid-day meal in a hotel which had an altar at one end of the room, as the local church had been either damaged or destroyed, so church services were held there.

Being inside a house or shelter that was hit did not always mean instant death. People were often buried under the rubble and had to be dug out by ARP rescue parties, as this report from 1943 shows:

When a rescue party set to work to see who might be buried in the debris of a demolished house, they were warned of life to be saved and guided to their mark by the notes of 'God Save the King' sung at the top of his voice by a little boy of 6. It turned out that he was trapped under the staircase, where he had to stay for six hours until rescued. He was singing most of the time. His rescuers asked him why. He told them: 'My father was a collier, and he always said that when the men were caught and buried underground they would keep singing and singing and they were always got out in time.'

Christine Pilgrim from Peckham: 'Later, people stopped using cellars, they realised that if the house was hit you'd be buried down there, under the rubble, so we used to go to the street shelter up the road. I remember in one heavy raid a neighbour who was an Irish lady, I never realised she was a Catholic before, loudly repeating her prayers – "Hail Mary" – over and over, as if she was trying to shut out the noise. I just wanted her to shut up!'

The raids, with their noise and the constant danger, could indeed have dreadful effects on older people, but most children took them in their stride. In *The City That Wouldn't Die*, Richard Collier relates the following story. It is the early hours of 11 May 1941, and London's worst raid is at its height:

Near Millwall Outer Dock, Station Officer Bernard Belderson and a police sergeant met a small girl skipping unconcernedly along the road, eyes glistening with excitement, only a coat thrown over a thin night-dress. When she answered that she was just having a look around, Belderson expostulated: 'But look, there's a German aeroplane up there.'

'Huh,' she grunted. 'That's all right. That square-headed bastard couldn't hit a haystack.'

David George was in Ealing: 'Once a stick of bombs landed in the road next to us. When my mum came to wake me up I was lying on the floor next to my bed – the impact of the bombs must have tumbled me out of my bed – but I'd slept through it all!'

In 1943 one woman air-raid warden wrote:

the vast majority [of children] did not seem to be much affected. I have seen some children who would stand shivering and sweating in a shelter, and no amount of coaxing would induce them to utter a word. But most of them slept soundly, and only showed a healthy excitement. Every morning one was besieged by crowds of small boys and girls: 'Got any shrapnel, Miss? Billy got a shell cap yesterday – give me one, Miss.' Collecting shrapnel and bits of bombs was more the rage than the vanished cigarette card had been.

The original caption for this photograph reads: 'In one of the countless tip-and-run raids in which the Luftwaffe harried Britain's coastline this 14-year-old schoolboy worked all through the night rescuing buried people.' (HMSO)

Charles Harris recalls the craze: 'I used to collect shrapnel – my best piece fell down in the road beside me when I was running to the shelter – it was red hot. I also had a lump of parachute cord off a land mine, it was about an inch thick, made of green silk.' George Parks of Deptford also remembers collecting shrapnel: 'After a raid the kids'd all pour out and come back with loads of shrapnel. My old man'd say: "What you effing got there? Get rid of it." But I always kept the best bits!'

It could be dangerous – in *Children of the Blitz*, Robert Westall tells of one 14-year-old civil defence messenger who kept an unexploded incendiary as a souvenir:

One day I took it to school in the saddlebag of my bike and showed it to my friends there. It passed from hand to hand and during assembly one of the 'wags' had to test it by dropping it on the floor. The bomb detonated and in the chaos

Kent schoolboys put on a shrapnel exhibition to raise money for the war. (Kent Messenger Newspaper Group)

that resulted the hall filled with smoke and the boys evacuated it in record time to reassemble in the courtyard. . . . It was eventually put out, but left a crater in the parquet flooring and damaged the honours list.

The bombing tended to happen in phases; after the Battle of Britain it was mainly, but not solely, at night, and the targets changed. Sometimes the Luftwaffe bombed cities, sometimes ports and factory towns; there might be a massive force of bombers, but sometimes only a few came over, or even just one. Towns all over England, Scotland, Wales and Northern Ireland were attacked; particularly badly hit were London, Manchester, Liverpool, Portsmouth, Plymouth, Coventry, Birmingham, Hull, Clydeside and Bristol. Iris Smith:

Bristol got a lot of bombing, near us they were after the railway; about ten or twelve houses along, three houses were destroyed, and another one over the back of us. You never knew what you were going to find when you came out of the shelter in the morning. We were often without water, as the bombs burst the mains, then we went and queued up outside the nearest house that still had water, and carried home buckets full of water. Even hot water was short then, you could only have 6 inches in the bath, and we all took it in turns to use the same water. Later I became a fire-watcher, it wasn't nice coming home in the morning at six o'clock – I never knew if I was going to see my family or my house again.

The damage was not just from high-explosive bombs. On 29 December 1940 the City of London was attacked with incendiaries: over 1,500 fires were started in what came to be called 'the Second Great Fire of London'. June Fidler from Peckham: 'A stick of incendiaries fell down our road. We were in the Anderson at the time. One came through our roof, it burnt my bed and all my toys – I'll always remember that terrible smell of burning. Mum couldn't get a new bed, we had to borrow one from a woman whose daughter was evacuated. You just couldn't replace toys – you *never* lost your Ludo board!'.

Dover and the other coastal towns nearby were regularly shelled by long-distance guns on the French coast, and from June 1944 Britain came under attack from the V-weapons.

'V' in this case stood for *Vergeltungswaffen*, German for 'reprisal weapon'. First came the V1, which had many nicknames: flying bomb, flybomb, doodlebug and buzzbomb were the most common. It was a pilotless aircraft, powered by a pulse-jet motor and containing an explosive warhead in its nose-cone. Cheaply built, the V1s were launched from sites in France and flew until their engines cut out, whereupon they went into a dive and exploded on impact. Their greatest advantage was that they could be launched day or night, in any weather; their biggest disadvantage, that they flew in a straight line, which made them fairly easy to shoot down, either with anti-aircraft fire, or by fighter aircraft. Later the fighters learned how to tip the V1s over so that they exploded harmlessly in the fields. Most were shot down, but the air-raid sirens gave warning of those that got through. People soon learned that you were safe as long as you could hear their engine, a very distinctive sound. Vivien Hatton: 'I remember watching the doodlebugs being shot down at Addington. The engines made an awful noise, but it was when they stopped you had to worry, that's when they'd come down with a whooosh. We had a French teacher, Miss Pike, who, when they came over, used to say "You can go out into the corridor, if you like", but we didn't want to appear afraid so we'd stay where we were.' And people learned other tricks; Christine Pilgrim: 'With the V1s you started counting the moment the engine cut out. You didn't always hear the blast, but you knew if you got to twenty you were all right.'

From the time the first V1 landed on Bethnal Green on 15 June 1944, up to 100 a day were sent over, almost up to the end of the war.

Sylvie Stevenson remembers:

When the doodlebugs started coming over, we used to do practices in school – if you couldn't get to the shelter quick enough you had to throw yourself down on the ground. All the corridor windows were bricked up. Once a doodlebug came down near the school; I was off sick that day, when we heard it we all ran into the street. The women were outside saying, 'Where did it land', then someone said, 'The school!' – they all just ran there, but luckily it was OK. The next day all the kids were replaying what happened, 'We threw ourselves on the floor like this!' they kept telling me, and then showed me!

The V2 was a real rocket. Carrying about 1 ton of explosives, it was launched straight up into the upper atmosphere; then, turning, it came straight down, faster than the speed of sound. It was a truly awful weapon, very accurate, and so fast that it could be neither seen nor heard – the explosion was the first anyone knew of it. The first two landed in Chiswick and Epping on 8 September 1944, and they continued to come until 27 March 1945, just a few weeks before Germany surrendered. Unlike the V1, the V2 had few nicknames; perhaps it was just too frightful.

During the war almost 8,000 British children were killed, and a similar number seriously wounded, as a result of enemy action.

One last story of the bombing from David George tells more about the survival of pre-war manners than anything else:

I remember one air raid vividly – I was in the garden of my home, and I had a bag of plums, probably from my nan's garden. Suddenly the sirens went and the German planes came over – you could see the bombers in the sky. My mother told me to get inside, she said: 'Mister Hitler is after your plums!' I ran inside so fast I slipped on the lino and crashed against a door frame, splitting my forehead open – I still have the scar today!

In the midst of the bombing 'he' is still referred to as 'Mister' Hitler!

PETS

Then as now, many children kept pets, and for them the Blitz created particular problems. Most animals hate loud bangs and flashes. Each year on 5 November, Bonfire Night, pet owners are reminded to keep dogs, cats and so on safe indoors – imagine what it was like for animals in the Blitz! The problem was even worse because horses were widely used to pull delivery vehicles, or on farms – it was estimated that there were almost 1.25 million working horses in Great Britain at the time.

Pets were not allowed in public shelters, so owners were advised to take them into their own gas-proof rooms or shelters; those who did not have their own shelter were told to try to send their pets to friends in the country, or, failing that, to have them put down. Christine Pilgrim remembers her pet dog: 'We had a cocker spaniel, it was dreadfully upset because it wasn't allowed to come down in the shelter with the rest of us.'

Gas masks were produced for horses, but were expensive at about £2 each. In the First World War, some message-carrying dogs had been fitted with masks, but they had to be specially trained to wear them; in the Second, there were no gas masks for cats or dogs. Although gas-proof boxes and kennels were available, the RSPCA did not recommend them as air had to be pumped in and, should its owner be injured, the animal would suffocate or die of starvation. The RSPCA recommended the following: 'If gas is used put your dog or cat in their sleeping basket (the sleeping basket could be covered with another of similar size inverted over it), take both into your shelter and put over the animal an ordinary woollen blanket that has been soaked in plain water or a solution of permanganate of potash. Only do this when the rattle warning for gas attack has been given.'

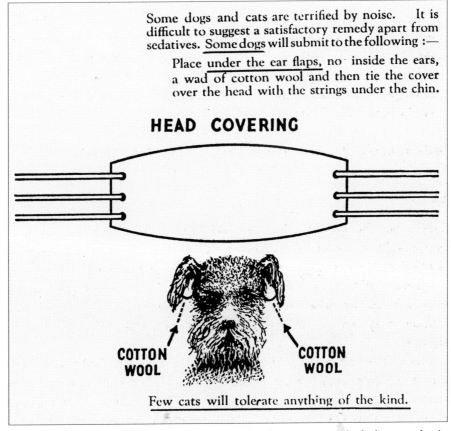

Head-covering for a dog from an RSPCA leaflet. The idea was to cover the dog's ears so that it could not hear the bombs. (RSPCA)

IMPORTANT!
NO. OF PERSONS SLEEPING IN THIS HOUSE
DOG / CAT
(Cross out whichever is inapplicable)

ALSO **IN**
HOUSE
HIS   BED   IS

(State location of bed as exactly as possible)

Issued by

The National Canine   The Royal Society for the
Defence League,   Prevention of Cruelty
Victoria Station House,   to Animals,
S.W.I.   105, Jermyn Street, S.W.I

'Dog/cat in house' poster. This would help rescuers to find the animals in the case of a bomb hitting the house. (RSPCA)

Similarly, birds's cages should be covered with 'a blanket soaked in water or bicarbonate of soda solution'.

The government set up a wartime organisation, the National ARP for Animals Committee (NARPAC), which included groups such as the RSPCA and the PDSA. NARPAC street animal guards, all of whom worked voluntarily, kept registers of all animals in their area. A numbered disc was supplied to each animal on the register, enabling the owners of lost or injured animals to be traced. In 1942, the Greenwich deputy ARP controller said: 'After a raid 7,000 animals were rescued or found homeless, over half that number had to be put to sleep because they had no NARPAC discs.'

Air raids were not the only wartime problem for pet owners; food for pets was in extremely short supply. Alternatives were suggested: dog biscuits and gravy, boiled rice and gravy, brown bread crisped in the oven, horsemeat, parts of cow/sheep not eaten by humans. One complete meal recipe for dogs was: '5–6 ounces of stale bread, toasted. Mix with 3–4 ounces of chopped cabbage, cauliflower, brussels sprouts, turnip or other green leaves, mashed and boiled for about 15 or 20 minutes. Moisten the mixture with soup or gravy made from bones or scraps from the table.' There were even calls in Parliament for a small milk ration for cats.

For pet birds, a suggested diet was stale bread crusts, brown or white, toasted and thoroughly dried, along with grated carrots and then mixed into a crumbly state by adding milk. For green food, lettuce and dandelion were recommended. For bird tables there were many suggestions, including: 'Soft bacon rind free from fat (which is too useful for cooking purposes to be fed to birds) may be minced finely, this will be appreciated by blackbirds and thrushes.'

A further problem was the black-out; road deaths for dogs and cats, as well as humans, soared.

FOUR

School

At the outbreak of war all schools were closed for one week. In Evacuation areas, the children who had stayed put presented a special problem. For them no organised schools were open and although efforts of various kinds were made the problem remained. Most teachers had been evacuated with their schools – for instance, only 300 teachers remained in the whole of London.

However, the school buildings had not been left unused. Families who were 'bombed out' had to be rehoused, but this could take several weeks, so short-term rest centres and feeding centres were set up, and school buildings, being very suitable for the task, were often used. Other schools were converted into auxiliary fire stations, emergency ambulance stations, rescue party depots and so on. D.J. Ryall of

School building used as stretcher party depot. (Lewisham Local Studies Library)

New Cross had been evacuated from Brockley Central School: 'over the following six months many of the children came back to London. The school had ceased to function so those that returned had to find others which were set up like Coll's Road, Peckham.'

In December 1939, London schools began to reopen, but not enough of them – of the 900 elementary schools, only 120 opened their doors again to pupils, although by early 1940 over half the schoolchildren of London were back. Of these, 34,000 were taught in shifts in the remaining schools, but 100,000 had to be tutored at home: groups of children would assemble at a given place, usually one of their homes, and the teacher would come to them, normally twice a week. At first, groups were to be no bigger than six because of the danger of bombing, but later the number grew to twelve, and then to twenty. Charles Harris from Chingford had home tuition:

> We had about four hours a week of education, but not in school. About six of us used to go round to Roy Kay's house, his mother had the teacher there for about two hours, we did the same at the Hintons'.
>
> Later on I went to the secondary school – when the sirens went you could only leave school if somebody came for you. Roy lived near the school and Mrs Kay came for him, she said to me: 'You can come as well if you like.' We were cutting across the field when we saw a German bomber coming over, ever so low – we could see the pilot – we all dived into the hedge!

Iris Smith from Bristol remembers: 'My little sister didn't go to school. Twice a week the teacher used to go round to No. 35 and my sister and some other children would go there. My sister was younger than the other children so she didn't do very well.'

More schools were reopened, or teachers and pupils shared a school's premises with the emergency services, but because children were allowed back only when air-raid shelters had been provided, the process took time. Margaret Woodrow started her first teaching post a few days before the outbreak of war. 'The air-raid shelters were not finished so we teachers were employed at the Town Hall preparing ration books. Later, half the pupils came for lessons in the morning and half in the afternoon. Teachers set homework to be done in the off part of the day.'

Margery Neave taught in Middlesex, she remembers the shelters:

> We had two air-raid shelters in the school, they were narrow tunnels under the earth running at right angles to each other, so the Headmistress could stand at

the corner and shout instructions both ways at once! There were roughly made wooden benches on each side and just enough room to walk down the middle. You can imagine the lessons! One thing we could do was sing.

Whenever the air-raid warning was sounded, we picked up our gas masks in their cardboard boxes and filed down into the shelter in an orderly way, each teacher with her own class, and there we had to stay, sometimes for many hours – past lunch time and sometimes past end of school time – until the all clear sounded.

Carol Smith remembers sheltering in her school at Dunstable:

Once when my little brother and I were on our way to school, the warning went. We had an argument, I said we were three-quarters of the way there and should go on. He wouldn't come and went up the chalk cutting to watch – there was a hut there. A German plane came up the A5, by then I was in the air-raid shelter at school. When the plane dropped his load, I remember the headmaster, a very nice man, Mr Underwood, he said, 'Don't worry, it's only a lorry dumped his load of bricks.' I thought, 'What sort of fools does he take us for?' I was 13 years old at the time.

As school buildings once again became available, they were re-opened as 'emergency schools', responding to the needs of the neighbourhood – thus a building that had been a secondary school might be re-opened as an emergency primary school. In 1940 emergency schools were organised as all-age schools; during the following year they became more specialist, until by the end of 1942, in London there were 43 emergency central, 96 emergency senior and 109 emergency junior schools.

As the Blitz progressed, however, a growing number of schools fell victim to bombs. In London 150 were destroyed and over 200 damaged, and the shortage was never fully resolved. Joyce Somerville from Brockley remembers her school:

I attended Wallbutton Road School in 1942 aged 9. When I joined the school we only used part of it; the hall upstairs was about half the size it should have been as it had been bombed and had been bricked up, with a curtain across to cover the rough bricks. We used three classrooms on that floor and one on the ground floor which had windows which had been bricked up to make it into a shelter against air raids. One part of the school was taken over by the ambulance service and another was given over to the heavy rescue service.

Iris Smith describes her schooling:

Once we couldn't go our usual way to school because there was an unexploded
bomb. We only went for half a day during the bombing. We had to share the
school with other children, half went in the morning and the other half went
in the afternoon – I went in the morning. Once an incendiary bomb came
through the ceiling of the biology lab, and another time a bomb went off in the
playground – luckily it was at night or who knows how many of us might have
been killed.

In the Reception areas the task of finding appropriate buildings to make into
temporary schools proved most difficult. At first much work was done outside,
but slowly accommodation was found. In 1939 it had been decided to build
a series of camp boarding schools, outside the danger areas. Thirty-one were
started, and by early 1940 many were ready to take what we would now call
secondary age children. This is a description of the camps from 1941:

The Camps are all in rural areas, standing on large sites of 20–40 acres, carefully
selected with regard to drainage and water supply. The buildings, constructed
of cedar wood on concrete foundations and roofed with shingles, have a pleasing
appearance. They generally include four classrooms; two other rooms to be
used as practical rooms; a hall, which can also be used for teaching purposes,
complete with stage; a large dining-room, together with a kitchen, staff rooms,
a store, and, not least important, a tuck shop. As a rule, five dormitories are
provided, each equipped with two-tier iron bedsteads, with a small room for a
teacher at each end. A lavatory block with baths, showers and a drying room;
a hospital block for about seven patients and a nurse; quarters for the Camp
School staff and self-contained flats for the Headmaster and the Camp Manager,
complete with equipment. Central heating by radiators and electric lighting
make it possible to use the Camps continuously throughout the year.

Early in the war the use of hand-bells and whistles, standard for teachers on
playground duty, was banned (hand-bells were part of the poison gas warning
system, and whistles to warn of falling incendiary bombs). Another big change
was in holidays. It was quite normal for schools to work through to mid-August
and then have just two weeks's summer holidays, but to get ten weeks's holiday
at Christmas! This was to save fuel needed for lighting and heating. June Fidler
from Peckham tells of other shortages:

With all the shortages the exercise books were cut in half with a guillotine or whatever and we had half of one each, they did the same with the pencils. We normally had to write with a dip pen using ink which a class monitor mixed up from powder, it was horrible stuff, but it ran out so we had to do all our writing with our half-pencils. And the textbooks, what there were of them, four or five of us had to share, but I hear it's the same today, so some things don't change.

Schools with cellars put them to use as air-raid shelters. Others either had purpose-built air-raid shelters in the grounds, or converted a ground-floor room to a shelter by having all its windows bricked up. Air-raid practices were common, as were gas mask practices. Here is a report from 1941: ' "Run, rabbits, run," calls the teacher, and instantly some 20 or 30 little people disappear, leaving no signs of their presence but an odd foot or two sticking out from beneath the desks. No, it is not a new game for the infants's school: at least, it may be a game for the children, but it is something more than that – it is practice in taking cover against sudden air attack.'

Most raids were at night, but there were also many in daylight, especially during the first year of the war, and lessons would be disrupted as everyone

School gas-mask practice (Kent Messenger Newspaper Group)

Rescuers dig in the rubble at Sandhurst Road School, Catford, after it had been hit by a 500 kg bomb at lunchtime on 20 January 1943 – thirty-eight children and six teachers died. (Lewisham Local Studies Library)

filed down to the shelter. At first it was thought that the raids would be over very quickly, but in fact warnings often lasted for several hours, so teachers had to think up ways to stop the children becoming bored and restless. Community singing was the most obvious distraction, to which were added story-telling, guessing games such as 'I Spy', charades and recitations. Sometimes a school would put on a show with each class taking its turn in entertaining the others: scenes from plays, music solos. As the war went on, shelters became better equipped with lights and heating and some lessons could be carried on there.

Schools were often hit, although with most of the bombing happening at night there were few casualties. The results of daytime raids, however, could be awful: at lunchtime on Wednesday 20 January 1943 a Focke Wulf 190 fighter-bomber, one of a group carrying out a tip-and-run raid, dropped its 1,100-pound (500 kg) bomb on Sandhurst Road School in Catford. No sirens were sounded. Teachers, hearing the plane circling overhead, had begun to lead the children down into the shelters. The bomb went through the wall of the school and exploded about a minute later in the dining hall, demolishing the centre of the building. Being lunchtime, many children were in the hall, and it was here that the casualties were at their highest – in all, thirty-eight children and six teachers were killed. The headteacher, Margaret Clarke, later said: 'The only question the children were asking was "How can I help, Miss?" They took home the younger ones, tore up their clothing to bind the injuries and even helped in the rescue work – a grim job for youngsters of 14 and 15.'

When an LCC nursery school was destroyed by an incendiary bomb, the children were luckily not there at the time. The school was later evacuated to the village of Crockham Hill in Kent where, on the morning of Friday 30 June 1944, it received a direct hit from a flying bomb. Twenty-two of the thirty children and eight of the eleven members of staff were killed. It is a chilling example of the devastation caused by these weapons that the last bodies were not recovered until two days after the incident.

Overall, the effects on children's education cannot be understated. D.J. Ryall's experience was typical: 'Due to the war my year did not complete their education past 16 although we all intended to stay on 'til 18. I left from Lingfield aged 15½ in 1940.' The disruption was not always unwelcome, Iris Smith explains: 'I did my school certificate during the war. We had done our mock certificates before and I had done quite well – I kept hoping the sirens would go – if they went while we were taking it they would have accepted our mock marks and I would have passed – but there wasn't a sound.'

FIVE

Shortages

One of Britain's great advantages in time of war is that the British Isles are exactly that – islands. This makes invasion far more difficult. But it also has a drawback: most of the food and raw materials that Britain consumes have to be imported by sea from other countries. In 1939, like an army laying siege to a castle in a medieval war, Germany put Britain under siege, using U-boats to sink merchant ships bringing in food, oil, petrol, wood, and many other vital materials. Losses were huge – over half of all the British merchant ships at the beginning of the war had been sunk by the end of it, and Britain came closer to losing the war to the U-boats than in any other way.

The situation was made worse by the need for vast amounts of material for the war effort. Thousands of aircraft, tanks, ships and guns had to be manufactured and millions of tons of steel were required, as well as rubber, oil and petrol. And the soldiers, sailors and airmen needed hundreds of thousands of uniforms, stitched from miles of cloth.

Scarce materials had to be conserved, so the government introduced a series of special measures. Petrol was a particular problem and the use of private cars was drastically cut back. Ration coupons for petrol were available solely to those using their cars for war work. Other materials

The Squanderbug – a sort of German agent insect that encouraged people to waste money on things they didn't need. (HMSO)

soon followed: rationing was introduced first for food, later for clothes, and even for furniture. Besides rationing, the government introduced other methods of saving scarce materials, campaigning to cut down on the unnecessary use of goods. Slogans such as: 'Is your journey really necessary?' became catch-phrases. A cartoon character, the squanderbug – a kind of large beetle, with Hitler's hair – was shown encouraging people to buy things they did not need.

Shortage signs were seen everywhere: 'No sweets', 'No cigarettes' and, outside pubs, 'No beer', were common sights. Another cartoon character appeared; answering to the name of Chad, he was drawn everywhere peering over a wall, with a question mark over his head and the question 'Wot, no . . . ?' The missing word could be any one of a thousand things.

Mike Bree from Cornwall:

The whole thing started slowly (our first Christmas we hardly saw a difference – they did allow us that!), then gathered momentum until the 'darkest days' – and then the 'shortages' went from bad to worse as the things we had started the war with – clothes, household goods, etc. – wore out, were broken or lost, or were taken from us by the Luftwaffe, or by our own government, by regulation or by appealing for 'the war effort'. Waste of all kinds was strongly discouraged,

Ino toilet soap advertisement from 1942. Make-up was very hard to obtain: powdered starch was used as face powder, and beetroot juice as rouge. Even hair grips were scarce.

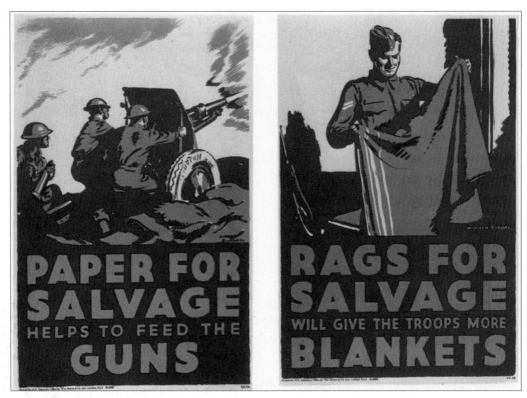

Two of the many posters urging people to save their salvage. (HMSO)

every bit of metal, glass, cardboard, wood, rubber, wool, everything, was vital. Even our town hall had to lose its courtyard railings, as did so many public and private buildings – there was hell to pay when they were found years later, rusting and forgotten in railway sidings.

People had to make things last, but the longer the war went on the more worn out things became. Vivien Hatton remembers a trip to an ice-rink near the end of the war: 'We had to borrow the skates from the rink. They had holes in!'

SIX

The Food Front

DIG FOR VICTORY

To cut down on the need for imports every inch of space was used to grow food, even the moat around the Tower of London; some tennis courts and even cricket pitches were ploughed up. People were encouraged to 'Dig for Victory', and this was an activity in which children could be particularly useful. Often children would take over some part of their garden for vegetable growing; even the earth covering the Anderson shelter was used for growing food.

The Ministry of Agriculture and Fisheries issued a series of 'Dig for Victory' leaflets, giving tips not only on growing vegetables, but also on preserving food, making jam, etc.

RATIONING

The pre-war government had created a Food Department in 1939, with the threat of war in mind, and in September of that year the National Register was set up to keep track of the population. Using this information, the government supplied everyone with a ration book. Because it was felt that different groups of people needed different types or amounts of food – for instance, children received orange juice and cod liver oil, and younger children got extra milk – there were several different

'Grow More Food' leaflet dated November 1939. Inside it says: 'Wanted 500,000 more allotment growers'.

ration books. The main types were the Adult book, which was a buff colour, the Baby's book, which was green, and the Junior book, which was blue. On 1 November 1939, it was announced that butter and bacon (or ham) were to become the first goods to be put 'on the ration': 4 ounces of each per person per week, beginning on 8 January 1940. At the end of December 1939 the government further announced that sugar was also to be rationed – 12 ounces a week. In March 1940 meat became rationed, not by amount, but by value: 1s 10d (9p) worth per person per week. In May the production of non-essential consumer goods was restricted. By now the Food Department had become the Ministry of Food (the MoF), under Lord Woolton, who gave his name to the Woolton Pie (p. 50).

By Christmas 1940, tea, that great British staple, had been rationed to 2 ounces a week, and the sugar ration was cut to 8 ounces. Worse, it was announced that after Christmas there would be no more bananas, and no fresh or tinned fruit would be imported, except a few oranges, as the shipping space was so badly needed for the war effort.

In January 1941 the value of the meat ration was dropped: first to 1s 6d (7.5p), then to 1s 2d (6p), and again in June to 1s (5p). It is said that Winston Churchill enquired why people were complaining about the size of the meat ration; when shown it he remarked that it would be quite enough for him – he thought it was the amount for one meal, it was actually a week's worth! Jam, marmalade, syrup and treacle went on the ration from 17 March 1941 at 8 ounces per person. Cheese was next: in May the weekly ration was set at 1 ounce, which was increased to 2 ounces from the end of June (registered vegetarians were entitled to extra cheese instead of meat). In July the sugar ration was doubled for a month to encourage people to make their own jam using the large amount of fruit available at that time of the year; children helped with the picking. Later, shortages led to the introduction of milk rationing.

In July 1942 the tea ration for under-5s was abolished, but for most children the worst blow came later that month when sweets were rationed; everyone was allowed 2 ounces a week, raised in August to 3 ounces, and in the same

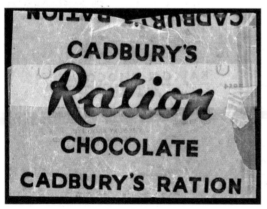

Cadbury's ration chocolate wrapper. Sweet rations of 3 ounces a week meant that large chocolate bars became a thing of the past

month biscuits were put on points, as were syrup and treacle. An element of choice was introduced. As well as the coupons for specified rationed goods, each ration book contained a number of points coupons. While some items of food were 'put on points', the points coupons could be used to buy any items on points. Even before rationing, sweets had been hard to get. A letter from Alan Miles (14 August 1941) 'I am thankful for the sweets [you sent] as you can't get a sweet in Hartland for any money.' June Fidler: 'We got 2 ounces of sweets a week on rations – we used to buy the smallest sweets we could, pear drops and so on, so that you got a lot of them.' Special ration-sized chocolate bars were produced, and Barratts introduced the Ration Bag, 'containing sweets, nuts, pop-corn, etc.'; this later became the Jamboree bag. Shortages of milk meant that milk chocolate was difficult to get – for instance, Rowntrees produced a plain chocolate Kit-Kat in a blue wrapper. Children tried various ways to get round the rationing. Derek Dimond describes one: 'The worst thing was the shortage of sweets, we used to buy Victory V lozenges which were off rations.' Other alternatives included 'Imps', tiny black lozenges which were extremely hot – they too were off rations.

Babies first, please!

So many little mites depend for their health – and often their very lives – on Nestlé's Milk.

For thousands of delicate babies Nestlé's Milk is essential – it is the only food they can take. In countless difficult cases, when nothing else would do, Nestlé's Milk has worked what seemed a miracle.

But the supplies of milk are short today, and in our effort to meet the needs of those anxious mothers who have delicate babies to feed we seek your help. Please do not ask your grocer for Nestlé's Milk unless you need it for your baby.

Nestlé's Milk is goodness, nothing but goodness : pure, creamy milk taken with all its vitamins, all its fats, and so prepared that the frailest baby system can digest it easily and absorb all its nourishing goodness.

Issued by Nestlé's Milk Products Ltd.

*Nestlés's Milk advertisement – you won't find adverts today which say 'please do **not** ask your grocer for Nestlé's milk'!*

In August 1942 the cheese ration was increased to 8 ounces. Ration books issued in June 1943 included personal points for sweets and chocolates. Barbara Courtney: 'I remember we used to go to the shops to get our food rations, 2 ounces of this, 2 ounces of that, then we'd share them. You'd swap your sugar ration for sweets, jam for sugar, and so on.'

Bread was not rationed, and nor were some other foods, such as potatoes and other root vegetables, but they were not always available. News would soon be passed round when a shop had something unusual in and a queue would soon form – during the war queuing became almost a national pastime, and here, too, children could help, both by spotting queues and by saving Mum a place in them.

The Ministry of Food produced a great deal of material on how to make the rations stretch. There were recipe books, and a series of newspaper articles, entitled 'Food Facts', which would give tips on cooking in wartime. There was even a radio programme, *The Kitchen Front*, broadcast every morning from Tuesday to Friday at 8.15 am.

Imported fruit, such as peaches and grapes, became almost impossible to get, and even if they were available, prices were extremely high. In 1944 street markets were selling pineapples for 5 guineas (£5.25) each, grapes at 16s (80p) for 1 pound and peaches at 2s (10p) each. Charles Harris: 'You never saw oranges. One Christmas, it must have been '43 or '44, Dad was in North Africa and he sent us a big basket of oranges. In those days the postman delivered on Christmas Day and they arrived Christmas morning. There were four really big ones – my two brothers, my sister and I had one each. My little brother was a baby – he had a green ration book, and with that you got orange juice.'

In Richmal Crompton's *William Carries On* (published in 1942), William asks his long-suffering mother for a lemon:

'Lemons?' said Mrs. Brown as if she could hardly believe her ears. 'Lemons? I hardly remember what they look like.'

'There's a picture of 'em in the 'cyclopaedia,' said William helpfully.

'I don't think I even want to remember what they look like,' said Mrs. Brown bitterly. 'No, I've not seen one for weeks.'

'If you wanted to get hold of one,' said William, 'how would you start?'

'I shouldn't,' said Mrs. Brown. 'I've given it up. After all, it's no use breaking one's heart over a lemon.'

'But suppose you had to have one,' said William, 'what would you do?'

'I shouldn't do anything,' said Mrs. Brown. 'What with onions and eggs, and icing sugar and cream, I've just given it up. There's nothing one can do.'

Although there were plenty of chickens in Britain when war broke out in 1939, the bulk of poultry feed was imported, making eggs hard to get. In the summer of 1942 powdered eggs were made available to domestic consumers. A packet, equivalent to twelve eggs, cost 1s 9d (9p). The Ministry of Food 'War Cookery Leaflet No. 11' was about powdered eggs, including instructions on 'How to reconstitute dried egg' – using one level tablespoonful of egg powder and two

"DRIED EGGS
are _my_ eggs –
my _whole_ eggs
and
nothing but _my_ eggs"

Dried eggs are the complete hen's eggs, both the white and the yolk, dried to a powder. Nothing is added. Nothing but moisture and the shell taken away, leaving the eggs themselves as wholesome, as digestible and as full of nourishment and health-protecting value as if you had just taken the eggs new laid from the nest. So put the eggs back into your breakfast menus. And what about a big, creamy omelette for supper? You can have it savoury; or sweet, now that you get extra jam.

DRIED EGGS build you up!

In war-time, the most difficult foods for us to get are the body-builders. Dried eggs build muscle and repair tissue in just the same way as do chops and steaks; and are better for health-protection. So we are particularly lucky to be able to get dried eggs to make up for any shortage of other body-builders such as meat, fish, cheese, milk.

Your allowance of DRIED EGG is equal to 3 eggs a week

You can now get one 12-egg packet (price 1 3) per 4-week rationing period — three fine fresh eggs a week, at the astonishingly low price of 1¼d. each. Children (holders of green ration books) get two packets each rationing period. You buy your dried eggs at the shop where you are registered for shell eggs; poultry keepers can buy anywhere.

Don't hoard your dried eggs; use them up — there are plenty more coming!

Note. _Don't make up dried eggs until you are ready to use them; they should not be allowed to stand after they've been mixed with water or other liquid. Use dry when making cakes and so on, and add a little more moisture when mixing._

FREE — DRIED EGG LEAFLET containing many interesting recipes, will be sent on receipt of a postcard addressed to Dept. 627E, Food Advice Service, Ministry of Food, London, W.1.

ISSUED BY THE MINISTRY OF FOOD (S.74)

Dried eggs pamphlet, issued by the Ministry of Food. Dried eggs were imported from America to save shipping space. (HMSO) of water, 'mix the egg and water and allow to stand for about five minutes until the powder has absorbed the moisture. Then work out any lumps with a wooden spoon, finally beating with a fork or whisk.' The leaflet went on to give various recipes, such as scrambled eggs, omelettes and cake mixtures, as well as 'English Monkey' and 'Mock Fried Egg'; these last two are reproduced below:

English Monkey

1 powdered egg
1 cup stale breadcrumbs
1 cup milk
half cup grated cheese
1 tablespoon margarine
half teaspoon salt
pepper

Soak the breadcrumbs in the milk. Melt the margarine in a pan, add the cheese and when melted add the soaked breadcrumbs and the egg (well beaten) and seasoning. Cook for three minutes. Spread on toast.

Mock Fried Egg

1 powdered egg
2 slices wheatmeal bread
salt and pepper

Beat the egg. Cut holes from the centre of each slice of bread with a scone cutter. Dip the slices quickly in water and fry one side until golden brown. Turn onto the other side, pour half the egg into the hole in each slice of the bread, cook until the bread is brown on the underneath side.

Early in February 1941 a standard wholemeal loaf, called the National Loaf was introduced. Far more of the wheat was used in making it, so there was less waste.

Several schemes were tried to make up for the shortage of meat. Sausages contained less and less real pork or beef; 'It's a mystery what's in these sausages,' says a character in the 1943 film, *Millions like Us*, 'and I hope it's not solved in my time!' By that year, horsemeat, or horse flesh as it was known, was commonly available, though rarely popular; also widely hated was whalemeat, which became available in 1945. On the other hand the war introduced the British public to the American creation, Spam, tins of which were a great treat. Rabbit was popular, especially in the countryside. Although fish was widely used as an alternative to meat, sometimes it was also scarce. New types of fish were tried out with little success, the most famous of which was Snoek (pronounced snook), an Australian fish, widely considered to be inedible.

People were encouraged to keep animals for food, and not just in the country. Sylvie Stevenson from Chingford in London:

Potato Pete's Recipe Book *issued by the Ministry of Food in 1945. Potatoes were not rationed, so recipe books like this one were issued to make potato-based meals more varied. The character on the front is, of course, Potato Pete himself. (HMSO)*

We had real eggs! We kept chickens, ducks, rabbits, and a goose, we kept them in the garage and in two sheds in the garden. We kept the rabbits for meat – there was one big rabbit called 'Blackie'; his cage was by the door and I used to see him a lot – when they cooked him I just couldn't eat my dinner – Mum was so cross. Dad bought the goose in about August, we were going to fatten it up for Christmas. He thought it was a male bird but it started laying eggs so we kept it, the eggs were lovely – they filled the whole frying pan! We had it for about two years until it stopped laying, so Dad killed it – I couldn't eat that either. The ducks were a disaster, there must have been half a dozen of them, Dad didn't clip their wings properly and they flew over the fence into next door's garden, the French windows were open and they went in – the neighbours were furious!

Communal feeding centres were set up. Their purpose was to serve low-cost, healthy meals, which used non-rationed food. Early in 1941 they were rechristened 'British Restaurants', and eventually there were over 1,000 of them set up around the country.

Children's party – the lady in uniform is an air-raid warden. A sign of food shortages is how pleased the children look with their apples. (Lewisham Local Studies Library)

SOME WARTIME RECIPES

All these recipes are taken from some of the many recipe books and leaflets printed at the time. Like many of the recipes of the period, they reflect the ingredients then available, or more accurately unavailable. While it can be fun to make and sample the food – some of them are quite good – I have to say that some of the recipes in this book taste quite appalling, and are here for historic rather than gastronomic reasons!

Woolton Pie

The ingredients of this pie can be varied according to the vegetables in season. Potato, swede, cauliflower and carrot make a good mixture. Take 1 pound of them, diced, three or four spring onions, if possible, 1 teaspoonful vegetable extract and 1 tablespoonful oatmeal. Cook together for 10 minutes with just enough water to cover, stirring occasionally. Allow to cool, put in a pie dish, sprinkle with chopped parsley and cover with a crust of potato or wheatmeal pastry.

Eggless, Fatless, Walnut Cake

4 cups flour
1 cup sugar
1 cup chopped walnuts
4 teaspoons baking powder
1 good cup milk
1 good pinch salt

Mix flour, sugar and chopped walnuts together. Add salt and baking powder, then the milk. It should be slightly wetter than an ordinary cake mixture. Leave to rise for 10 minutes. Bake in a greased tin in a slow oven until risen and brown.

Treacle Toffee Carrots

½ pound sugar
½ pound treacle
1 tablespoon vinegar
2 ounces margarine
bundle of fresh carrots

Melt the margarine in a strong saucepan and add the other ingredients (except the carrots). Bring to the boil, and boil steadily until a little dropped into cold water immediately becomes brittle.

Wash and scrape the carrots, and see that they are all well shaped. Dry them thoroughly, dip into the toffee as soon as it reaches the brittle stage. Pour the rest of the toffee into a greased tin to set firm.

Peek Freans's advertisement. Many wartime adverts demonstrated the effects of shortages.

THE YANKS ARE COMING

On 7 December 1941, Japanese aircraft attacked the US naval base at Pearl Harbor, and on 11 December Germany and Italy also declared war on the USA. Throughout 1942, US troops began to set up bases in Britain. They brought with them forgotten luxuries – ice cream, sweets, gum, and other shortage goods – and were followed everywhere by swarms of children on the off-chance that they might give some away. Derek Dimond was evacuated to Stanstead and remembers the US airmen:

Later in the war the Americans came and built an airfield. We used to watch the Marauders flying out: count them out and count them back, then work out how many hadn't returned. Sometimes they would come back damaged, on one wheel and so on, and crash on landing, if you were lucky there were flames – we were only children and thought that was very exciting, all the fire engines. I remember a Canadian plane crashing onto some pigs in a field and blowing up, we all collected up all the bits of aircraft for our shrapnel collections.

One popular saying that the kids used at the time was 'Got any gum, chum?' – the Americans used to have strip chewing gum and red apples, which you could only get from the United States. They used to go back home from Stanstead station and as they left they would throw them, and money, to us from the train.

Having plenty of everything – 'Over-sexed, over-paid and over here' was one popular description of US servicemen – meant that they were extremely

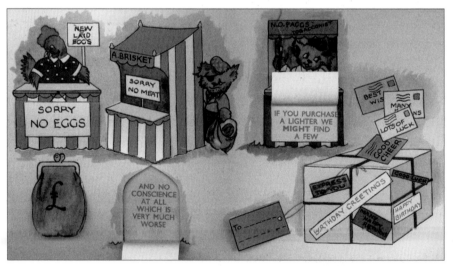

'Black Market' birthday card. Part of the pictures are cut away flaps with verses behind:
'2/6 each to you just step round the back [eggs],
For £10 I've a sirloin of beef in my sack,
If you use the black market you'll need a long purse
and no conscience at all which is very much worse
If you purchase a lighter we might find a few [cigarettes]
but there's plenty of greetings just specially for you'.

popular with children and young women, but loathed by everyone else, especially the British servicemen. This ill-feeling was taken so seriously by the government that a number of films were produced which showed British and US troops working together to beat the common enemy. Examples included Powell and Pressburger's *A Canterbury Tale* and Rattigan's *The Way to the Stars*, each of which also shows a sympathetic relationship growing between US airmen and British children.

The numbers of US troops, or GIs as they were called, built up as plans were laid for the Allied invasion of France (D-Day) in June 1944. June Fidler from Peckham:

US airmen with local children at a children's party in Wormingford, Essex, 1944.

I remember just before D-Day, all these huge American lorries were parked all along both sides of the road by Andover station, waiting for the US soldiers to come out of the station to take them to Portsmouth. We went and stood by the lorries talking to the troops. They gave us sweets and gum, it was my first taste of chewing gum. I also spoke to my first black man then, he was the driver. I went home and told my Nan; she said; 'They're not black, they're coloured.' That was the polite word in those days.

Not all the children were so friendly; Christine Pilgrim of Peckham recalls: 'We had a big American base near us, I remember seeing the GIs in their smart uniforms, some of the boys used to talk to them but we girls were very strictly warned off doing so, they were, after all, strangers.'

A FOOD FACTS QUIZ – CHRISTMAS 1941

Is Father as all-wise as he thinks he is? Does Mother know her P's and Q-pons? Here's the way to find out! Make a game of these questions round the fire this evening, and see whether the men or the womenfolk score the highest. The total score is 55; 50 is excellent; 40 not bad; anything less than 30 is – probably Father!

1 Which of these is the correct way to wash cooking fat so that it can be used again?
a) Pour boiling water over it; b) Rub through a fine sieve; c) Bring to the
    boil in water, pour into a bowl; when cool, lift off and scrape underneath;
    d) Hold it under running cold water.

Score 10

2 a) Is the following statement true or false? A child needs more meat than a man does.
b) What is the value of Points coupons A, B and C?

Score 5 for each question, full score 10

3 a) How many yolks and how many whites are in a ⅓ packet of dried eggs?
b) How many packets are you allowed this month?

Score 5 for each correct answer, full score 10

4 What is (or are) Rose Hips?
a) Name of a famous woman spy; b) An eastern dance; c) Pods of the wild
    rose, rich in Vitamin C; d) Name of a Russian folk song.

Score 10

5 How much priority milk are children under six allowed?

Score 5

6 Two of the following are provided by the Government for children under six years old. Which two?
a) Cocoa; b) Cod liver oil; c) Cornflour; d) Tomato juice; e) Orange juice

One correct answer 5, full score 10

PENALTIES: Ask Mother if she's filled in Section A at the top of page 35 of her ration book. If not she must deduct 5 from her total! Did Father offer anybody some of his sweet ration this Christmas? If not, he loses 5 from his score!

ANSWERS: **1** c). **2** a) True. A child needs actually more meat for its body weight than a man does. This is because meat is the kind of food (called protein) which is needed by the body for making new tissue and bones. b) A, 1; B, 2; C, 2. **3** a) 12 yolks and 12 whites – i.e. 12 whole eggs; 2 for adults, 4 for green ration book holders. **4** Pods of the wild rose. **5** 7 pints a week for green ration book holders. **6** b) and e).

SEVEN

Clothing

Children's clothes were far more formal in the 1930s and 1940s than they are today; their versions of trainers, track-suits and sports wear were strictly limited to the games field. For younger boys, perhaps 4 to 14 years old, normal dress consisted of short trousers, long socks, worn with sandals or boots, a shirt and tie (usually a school tie, often knitted), worn with a v-necked jumper and a jacket or school blazer. The whole outfit was finished off with a cap, usually from school or the Cubs. The illustrations to Richmal Crompton's *Just William* depict this perfectly.

For younger girls of school age, cotton frocks (dresses) in summer and gym-slips and blouses in winter were standard, worn with long socks or lisle stockings, sandals or shoes, topped with cardigans or jumpers, and either a school beret or a hat (straw in summer, felt in winter).

In winter, boys and girls would add overcoats or raincoats, with knitted woollen scarves, knitted gloves and, perhaps, wellington boots.

The passage from childhood to adulthood was very different at this time; at about 14 or 15 children suddenly became adults. The concept of the teenager appeared only in the 1950s as a reflection of the increased spending power of the age group brought about by post-war prosperity.

Fashions reflected this: teenage boys wore smaller versions of men's suits, which were sold with the option of long or short trousers;

This photograph is from a knitting book of the period. Clothes rationing meant that people were encouraged to make as many of their clothes as possible. This picture shows young children's sunsuits. (Practical Knitting Illustrated, Odhams)

This clearly shows the normal clothes for boys and girls up to the age of about 14. (*Knitting for All Illustrated*, Odhams)

Boy in shorts and 'sporting' jumper. (*Practical Knitting Illustrated*, Odhams)

similarly teenage girls began to wear smaller versions of their mothers's day dresses, and stockings instead of socks.

Some items of clothing were introduced, or made fashionable, by the war. Trousers, totally a male preserve before the war, were worn by more and more women, along with the 'siren suit' – what we might today call a boiler suit or overalls – and a head scarf. These were worn by factory workers and so wearers had the air of doing their patriotic duty; as such the clothes became fashionable, especially among the middle classes. Another item of wartime 'clothing' was the helmet: gentlemen's hatters, such as Dunn's, sold bakelite versions of the steel helmet, and every boy, including William, wanted their own. In *William and the Evacuees* (published in 1940), Richmal Crompton showed William in urgent need of 1*s* 6*d* – but penniless:

William wanted a tin hat. All the other Outlaws, all the other boys he knew, had tin hats of one sort or another, but it so happened that William was without either a tin hat or the money to buy one. Very inferior ones could be bought for as little as sixpence in Hadley, but William did not want an inferior one, and in any case he did not possess sixpence. The one he wanted cost one and six, but he was as likely to possess the moon as one and six, he told himself, adding with bitter sarcasm, 'a jolly sight likelier'.

RATIONING

Clothes rationing was announced on 1 June 1941 as coming into force immediately. Unlike food rationing, it was not primarily brought in as a result of shortages of raw materials, but in order to release factories and factory workers for war work. There were no separate ration books available, but people were told to use the spare coupons in their food ration books for the first year. Separate clothing ration books were first issued on 1 June 1942, these having red covers.

Rationing was extremely tight. The following suggested plans from a book printed at the time show how little you could get (children's outfits would be similar, with just a few changes, for example, girls socks instead of stockings).

Four-year Plan for a Woman's Wardrobe

First year
1 pair shoes
6 pairs stockings
10 ounces wool or 2.5 yards material
1 suit
1 overcoat
2 slips
1 blouse

Second year
1 pair shoes
6 pairs stockings
8 ounces wool or 2 yards material
1 silk dress
underwear: cami-knickers or vest and
knickers (2 or 3 pairs)
corselette or brassiere and
        girdle (2 or 3 pairs)

Third year
2 pairs shoes
6 pairs stockings
4 ounces wool or 1 yard material
1 jacket
1 skirt
2 cotton or silk frocks
2 slips
1 pair corsets
6 handkerchiefs

Fourth year
1 pair shoes
6 pairs stockings
6 ounces wool or 1.5 yards material
1 woollen housecoat or dressing-gown
underwear: cami-knickers or vest and
knickers (2 or 3 pairs)
corselette or brassiere and
girdle (2 or 3 pairs)
6 handkerchiefs

Evening-gowns are omitted from the plan since they are, in any case, not essential garments for most people. Special sportswear is also omitted on the same grounds. A macintosh is not included because umbrellas, which are unrationed, can be made to serve instead, used in conjunction with an old coat.

Four-year Plan for a Man's Wardrobe

First year
1 pair boots or shoes
6 pairs socks
1 suit (no waistcoat)
1 overcoat
collars, ties or handkerchiefs

Second year
1 pair boots or shoes
6 pairs socks
1 pair corduroy trousers
3 shirts (silk or cotton)
2 pairs of pants
2 vests
1 pair gloves

Third year
1 pair boots or shoes
5 pairs socks
1 suit (no waistcoat)
1 pullover
2 pairs of pyjamas

Fourth year
1 pair boots or shoes
6 pairs socks
1 overcoat, or unlined mackintosh and
vests
collars, ties or handkerchiefs
3 shirts
2 pairs of pants

Clothes rationing was a particular nightmare for parents. The scheme took little account of children growing out of their clothes. One early book had a section on this entitled: 'To eke out children's rations'; part of it ran:

Either through the school or through your local Women's Institute, you may be able to get in touch with other mothers and arrange to exchange your children's garments. You give a good dress or a suit, too small for your own daughter or son, and get in exchange a pair of shoes or a coat which can be worn for a year or more.

The question of school uniforms is already being tackled by the schools themselves. Uniforms are likely to be considerably simplified and, for the rest, an exchange system is almost certain to be worked out before the difficulties become formidable.

All sorts of clothing were in short supply. John Merritt:

In 1943 my family moved to Wokingham in Berkshire. I joined the 5th Wokingham Scouts and we used to have our meetings in a hall near St Paul's School. I do know that uniforms were in short supply, especially shirts and shorts and the 'lemon-squeezer' hats, which were much coveted. I did, however, get some green binding tape for my mum to make flashes for my socks, they of course fitted to the elastic garters that kept my socks up. Ninety-nine per cent of the boys wore short trousers. I didn't have a pair of long trousers until I left school at 15.

'This warm and serviceable set consisting of the jersey, beret, gloves and socks would appeal to any schoolgirl; especially if made in her school colours.' School uniform rules were greatly relaxed due to clothes rationing. (*Practical Family Knitting Illustrated*, Odhams)

As part of London's evacuation scheme the London Clothing Scheme was set up. Some of the children being evacuated came from very poor families indeed, and had few suitable clothes or shoes. Clothing stores were set up by the Women's Voluntary Service in reception areas, stocked partly by clothes supplied officially and partly by gifts. Children's parents paid according to what they could afford.

Clothes could be passed on and patched only so often before they became unwearable. At the end of 1942 it was announced that older children would receive extra clothing coupons in the following year's book; those born between September 1925 and December 1926 were to receive 10 extra coupons; between January and July 1927, 20 coupons; and from August 1927 up to the end of 1929, 30 extra. And if you think that was a bit complicated, there was more:

Children born after 1929 – who, when measured on or before 31st October 1943 are 5 feet 3 inches or more in height or who weigh 7 stone 12 pounds or more* (or need to wear boots or shoes of a size larger than 5½ in boys's or 3 in girls's) will receive 20 extra coupons (in addition to the 10 extra already supplied to them with their clothing book).

*Heights and weights must be measured without boots or shoes, jackets, waistcoats, and 2.5 pounds must be deducted to allow for weight of other clothing.

Mobile WVS clothing exchange. Clothes-rationing meant that new clothes were hard to get, so the WVS set up clothing exchanges, especially for children's clothes.

One thing never in short supply was bureaucracy, or 'bumf' (bum fodder – toilet paper).

MAKE DO AND MEND

To make the most of their existing clothes, the government encouraged people to 'make do and mend' (this meant patching and mending existing clothes) and to 'sew and save' (altering old clothes to make new ones). To this end the Board of Trade introduced the character of 'Mrs Sew and Sew': she was used in a series of advertisements to show how to 'turn two old dresses into a new one', and so on. There were meetings run by the Women's Institute or the WVS to give demonstrations and advice.

Not all the advice was particularly helpful. The Ministry of Information booklet 'Make Do and Mend', published in 1943, contains the following: 'Cutting-Down for the Children – Plus-fours will make two pairs of shorts for a school-boy. An old skirt will make one pair of knickers and a little play-skirt for a seven year old.', and, most baffling of all, 'Woollen stockings with worn feet can have the legs opened down the back seams and can then be made up into an infant's jersey. Bind it with ribbon at neck, sleeves and hem.'

If you were prepared to pay there was always the 'Black Market', which meant buying things illegally. But the goods were not always what they seemed. Vivien Hatton: 'Once we went to a market near Ludgate Circus, there were some wide-boys selling nylons without coupons. They were very expensive, ten shillings, I think, but we thought we'd got a bargain. When we got home and opened the boxes we found they had seams at the front – we'd been sold rejects!'

Mrs Sew and Sew, a character created for the Board of Trade to promote 'Make Do and Mend'. (HMSO)

Refoot your stockings

says **Mrs. SEW-and-SEW**

" As long as the legs are in good condition refooting can save many a pair of precious stockings," declares Mrs. Sew-and-Sew. " Here are some hints—if they don't go far enough a Make-do and Mend class will help you step by step."

Saves 1½ coupons a pair

REFOOTING SILK STOCKINGS
Undo the top hem of a cast-off stocking to give you material enough for a new foot. Open the seam. Use the foot of the same old pair for pattern.

Cut out the new foot with ¼" turnings. Seam the pieces for the new foot with close small stitches, following the pattern carefully.

Place the new foot over the old one and pin, folding the ¼" turnings. Sew down with small close hemming stitches.

Turn the stocking wrong side out and cut away the old foot, leaving only ¼" for turnings. Loop stitch the two turnings together and then hem down the loops to the stocking. Be sure to face the two turnings away from the silk.

★*Your Local Evening Institute, Technical College, or Women's Organisation is probably running a Make-do and Mend class where you can get help on all sorts of sewing problems. Ask at your Citizens' Advice Bureau.*

EIGHT

Doing Their Bit

Everyone was urged to do as much as they could towards the war effort – this was known as 'doing your bit'. Children were encouraged to become involved in war service from an early age. With younger children this mainly took the form of salvage – collecting waste products for re-use; today we would call this recycling.

Scrap materials collected included wastepaper, metal, bones, tinfoil, rubber, rags, bottles and jam-jars, as well as waste food and acorns for pig swill. Other collections included magazines and books for the forces, clothes for refugees and air-raid victims, and herbs, seaweed, horse-chestnuts, rose hips and nettles for use in making medicines.

Children's gas-mask march, Maidstone, May 1941. When the Germans failed to use gas in their raids, more and more people began to leave their masks at home. The government continued to encourage people to carry them. The two girls in front are carrying placards saying 'Carry your gas mask always with you'. Notice also the Scout, the Brownies, and the wartime queue, background right. (Kent Messenger Newspaper Group)

The government did its best to involve children in as many ways as possible. The following leaflet was issued in 1941 by the Ministry of Information. It sets out some of the many ways in which they could 'do their bit'.

**This leaflet specially concerns those
between 14 and 18 years of age**

YOU CAN HELP YOUR COUNTRY

THE DIFFERENCE between this war and previous wars is that now we are all in the front line in a struggle for the principles of freedom and justice and respect for the laws of God and honour amongst men. Whether we are in uniform or not, we are in the war. And no matter how young we are or how old we are there are jobs we can do for our country. This particular leaflet contains some suggestions for those who are between 14 and 18 years of age.

LOOK THROUGH this list of jobs to be done. Tick off any which you are already doing – and you'll probably be surprised to find how many there still are for you to tackle. Make up your mind which of them you would like to do or are able to do, and then get on with as many useful jobs as you can.

KNOW YOUR WAY ABOUT
If you're going to be handy in an emergency you should get to know everything about the district where you live. Where exactly are the Air Raid Shelters, the First Aid Posts, the Fire Stations, the Telephone Boxes, the Police Stations, the Footpaths and the Short Cuts? If you know where they are you may be able to save someone a few precious moments in an air raid. It is particularly important to know short cuts and footpaths. So get to know them now.

BEGIN AT HOME
a. If you want to be useful you should begin at home. You might make it your particular business to take charge of some of the Air Raid Precautions in your house – such as turning off the water and the gas when the sirens begin. To do that sort of job properly you should know where all the taps and connections are, and you should know how to deal with a leak of gas or a burnt-out electric fuse.

b. If you've got younger brothers and sisters, learn a few special games and tricks which will keep them from getting frightened during a raid.

c. Learn to cook a simple meal under emergency conditions.

d. Do your share of the odd jobs in the house, such as boot-cleaning, washing-up, black-out, mending and darning.

e. Make yourself the salvage-collector-in-chief in your house and see that all the wastepaper and metal and bones are regularly put aside for collection.

f. Try to get a plot of ground and grow extra vegetables.

LEND A HAND OUTSIDE

There are many jobs you can find to do in the district where you live. Here are a few.

a. Collect magazines and newspapers for the hospitals or the forces.

b. Go and help old people to grow vegetables in their gardens.

c. If you live in the country help the farmers at harvest-time, or lend a hand with the animals when you can.

d. Help elderly or invalid neighbours to put up an Air Raid Shelter.

e. Learn all you can about first-aid. The best way to do it is to join one of the organisations for boys and girls.

f. Join a group of young people in making splints and bandages or in knitting comforts for next winter.

g. Be sure you know how to use a telephone efficiently. You never know when you'll want to send a vital message quickly

h. Keep your eyes and ears open for other jobs; there are many other ways in which you can help.

SIX SIMPLE RULES

WORK HARD. If you're still at school remember that it's important to learn as much as you can if you want to become a useful citizen when you leave. If you're at work, put your back into the job, even if it means overtime. And if you are working so hard it means little time for leisure – never mind; you are doing your share to win the war.

BE CAREFUL WHAT YOU SAY. Like everyone else, you will hear things that the enemy mustn't know. Keep that knowledge to yourself – and don't give away any clues.

KEEP SMILING. There's a lot of worry and grief in the world – and you can lessen it by being good-tempered and considerate.

KEEP FIT. The fitter you are, the better able you will be to stand up to hard work. If you've left school, join a P.T. class and keep in good trim for victory.

SAVE ALL YOU CAN. Join a National Savings Group.

USE YOUR MIND and think for yourself.

Salvage advert from the Beano, *1941.*
(© D.C. Thompson & Co. Ltd)

IF IN DOUBT

If you are in doubt about what wartime job you should tackle, any clergyman or minister or the leader of any Boys' or Girls' Organisation will help you. If you are still at school, ask your teacher for advice. Then make up your mind and get on with the job. If you like to work with others, why not join one of the Boys' and Girls' Organisations and share in their activities? Some of them may be able to welcome you as guests for the time being.

At the end of 1941, the government decided to make it compulsory for all those aged between 16 and 18 to join some form of youth group; many, of course, were already members of one. Boards were set up to advise those who were uncertain which group would best suit them.

SCHOOLS

Some schools 'adopted' a ship or a military unit, knitted clothes and blankets for the men serving in it and also collected books and magazines to send to them. National Savings Groups were set up in thousands of schools where children would buy savings stamps, in effect lending their money to the country. Spitfire Funds

National savings card, stamp, and saver's badge. Inside the card it says: 'Here is a gift in season for the brighter days ahead'. Children formed savers's clubs at school, buying stamps every week – the card holds 30 stamps which were sold at 6d, 2s 6d, or 5s each.

were also set up, to enable the children of a school to save up to pay for their own Spitfire (or at least part of one). The following is a letter printed in the *Kentish Mercury* in February 1942: 'You may be interested to know that the children of Halstow Road School [in Woolwich] have for the last fortnight been bringing their pocket money to school, and, as a consequence, we have been able to send a cheque for eight guineas [£8.40] to the Chancellor of the Exchequer to help to provide life-saving jackets for our brave seamen.'

Secondary boarding schools usually had fire-fighting parties made up of staff and pupils. Other secondary schools organised fire-watching parties. Roy Coles went to school in Bristol: 'I also did fire-watching at school in 1944 and '45, four or five of the sixth form and teachers did it together – we stayed-over all night. I went to a boys's school, Cotham Grammar. Before the war we had all male teachers, but as it wore on the male teachers were called up and were gradually replaced by women and retired male teachers came back.'

In 1944, when the V1 attacks started, many schools in the south began using their pupils, on a rota basis, as raid spotters. The boy or girl on duty would usually sit at a desk set up outside the school with some work to do. On hearing a V1, they would look to see if it was coming in their direction; if it were, they could warn the school by an agreed method, such as the fire alarm, or a bell, so that pupils and

Girls of St Mark's School, Tunbridge Wells, knitting in the school air-raid shelter during an alert, March 1941. (Kent Messenger Newspaper Group)

V1 spotters outside their Kent school. (Kent Messenger Newspaper Group)

staff could all take cover. This cut down on the time which would be wasted by continually going to the shelters when a V1 flew past.

Outside school, besides working as individuals, boys and girls could join the many youth organisations which did war work, including some or all of the following.

CIVIL DEFENCE

Acting as messengers for the local police, the ARP, the local fire brigade, the Home Guard, and the Observer Corps. Working as telephonists, shelter marshals, control room orderlies, and gas-mask assemblers. Warning deaf neighbours of air-raid warnings or the All-clear, fire-watching, manning listening posts, painting kerbs and pavements white. Making camouflage nets, filling sandbags, painting and lettering helmets. Making and serving tea and sandwiches to civil defence workers.

IN HOSPITALS

Working as messengers, telephonists, stretcher-bearers, and cleaners, doing first-aid work, giving blood, and acting as patients for ambulance classes. Barbara Daltrey recalls wartime Windsor: 'I remember when war broke out, my mother and I made bandages out of old sheets. I went around the area collecting the sheets from houses – we were quite poor, and sometimes Mother said, "These sheets are better than ours, we'll swap them over."'

DIG FOR VICTORY

'Farmping' was an annual or weekend camp combined with working on the land; fruit-picking, harvesting and hop-picking.

Two boys with salvage metal. (Kent Messenger Newspaper Group)

SALVAGE

Collecting paper, scrap metal, etc., chopping wood for the aged and infirm. Collecting magazines and books for the forces.

WORKING WITH YOUNGER CHILDREN

Organising Christmas parties for younger children and collecting and mending discarded toys. Helping with evacuation.

The following are just some of the youth groups working during the war, many of which had, or created, bands to take the place of military bands at warship weeks, armistice parades, etc.

THE RED CROSS SOCIETY AND THE ST JOHN'S AMBULANCE BRIGADE

A leaflet issued by the Red Cross early in 1943 tells us that '10,000 boys and girls are already doing national war service with the British Red Cross Society'. It goes on to describe the ways in which they could help:

You will be trained to help the vital casualty and nursing services of the country in whatever way is most needed in your neighbourhood. It may be by doing part-time hospital duty so as to relieve hard-working nurses; it may be by helping in Civil Defence, so that you will have your job to do in an emergency; it may be by helping in children's nurseries, so that the mothers can make munitions; or it may be by helping in any of the services the Red Cross provides for the sick, wounded and prisoners. In all, you are urgently needed.

Children could join a cadet unit between the ages of 12 and 15, or a youth detachment from 15 to 20. They could become full members of the Red Cross as soon as they were 16 and had passed examinations in first aid and home nursing, or, for boys, in first aid only. The youth detachments learned not only first aid and home nursing, but also handicrafts such as book-binding, physical training and folk dancing! The syllabus also covered cooking, ARP training, hygiene and infant welfare. When trained, the youth detachments were equal in status to the adult detachments, equipped to do ward duty in hospitals, or with the blood transfusion service.

A similar situation existed in the St John's Ambulance Brigade's Cadet Nursing Division. Ken Kessie of Moreton: 'I used to go to St John's training, so they got me to work in Leasowe Hospital as a junior nurse I suppose you'd call it. We had all the blitz victims from Wallasey in there, I used to help bandage or stitch them up, it was a grim job for a 16-year-old!'

Red Cross leaflet from 1943 encouraging boys and girls to do war service. (British Red Cross)

SCOUTS

Sixty thousand Scouts were awarded the Scout National Service badge, which any Scout over the age of 14, who had passed his second-class tests, could win. The requirements of the badge were: an ability to write and carry messages; special knowledge of the local area; a capacity to deal with panic and keep discipline; and enrolment in some form of national service. There was also a Civil Defence Badge and the Scout War Service Badge. This entailed, among other things, signalling, first aid, unarmed combat, mapping, observation, weapons training and ARP work. Early in 1942, as a response to the compulsory registration of 16-year-olds, War Service Scout patrols were formed. Each was made up of six to eight boys, with one of them acting as the leader. The War Service patrols were intended to work with the ARP or the Home Guard. As uniforms were scarce, the boys were issued with special armbands.

Eric Chisnall was a Scout in Ipswich:

I was 9 years old when the Second World War was declared, and later became a member of the 14th Ipswich (St Augustine's) Scout troop.

Two incidents that occurred were connected with Emergency Service exercises. In the first I was acting as a casualty with a badly mutilated leg injury, supposedly bleeding very badly. I was located in a house about a mile or so from my home and I am sure that I must have bled to death as nobody came to attend to me. Eventually the occupant of the house sent me home as it was getting very late. It seemed a very long walk home in the black-out.

Presentation of a canteen van to the London borough of Deptford from children in Australia, 1942. Representatives of various youth groups, the Scouts, Cubs, Guides, Brownies and Boys's Brigade, are present, as well as service personnel. (Lewisham Local Studies Library)

Board of Trade 'Make Do and Mend' advert showing how to turn an old overcoat into a 'battle blouse'. (HMSO)

In the second, I was [acting as] a victim of mustard gas attack. A wide section of a road, Cliff Lane near some private houses and shops, just outside one of the entrances to our Hollywells Park, was the scene of this incident. A mobile unit arrived and set up in the middle of the road. A number of showers and canvas screens were erected. The treatment for this kind of gas contamination was to thoroughly wash down the affected skin. There were no half measures in this exercise, we had to strip off completely and pass through a series of these showers. I don't remember exactly what time of the year this exercise took place, but it probably wasn't winter because it was broad daylight. Nevertheless, I can still remember that the water was freezing cold.

One of the major jobs Scouts did was erecting Morrison shelters, 40,000 in all – the record was held by a Liverpool patrol which erected one in sixteen minutes. In Bethnal Green the local troop set up 5,000 three-tier bunks in Underground shelters in just nine months.

Experienced Scouts were also used, to a small extent, to instruct the Home Guard in field craft: tracking and camouflage. Country patrols worked with evacuees to show city children the ways of the countryside.

A Scout receiving rifle-training from Home Guard. Notice the War Service Scouts armband. (The Scout*)*

One story demonstrates the Scouts's tenacity; on 7 October 1940, the 36th Poplar troop lost their HQ to a bomb. By the middle of March they had rebuilt their meeting-room with boards dug out of the debris of the church next door, but it was blown to bits in another raid on 10 May. They had rebuilt it again by October. It then stood until the end of the war when, on VE night, the locals pulled down the fence the Scouts had put up around the hut to make a bonfire.

Michael Corrigan recalls his time as a Scout in Bristol:

When the war started I was 10 years old and a member of the 196th Cub pack. Unfortunately soon after the start of the war our cubmaster (Akela) was called up and the pack closed down.

I then had to wait until I was 11 to join the Scouts: the 26th Bristol (Northcote) troop. They consisted of three patrols – the Foxes, the Peewits and the Eagles – and were well into helping the war effort in any way they could. We had a regular wastepaper round and each Saturday one of the patrols would go out with the trek cart. We would distribute empty sacks to the households and collect full ones in return. We would then go back to our HQ and tip out all the sacks in our (now unused) Cub den and sort the paper into various grades. Newspaper, magazines, brown Kraft paper, and general writing and wrapping papers. As you can imagine this was a particularly dirty and messy job as people put all sorts of rubbish in the sacks besides paper and there we were, about eight boys up to their knees in a sea of paper, sorting it into more sacks for collection by one of the local paper mills for repulping and making into new paper.

Besides this, every time there was an urgent drive for metal, and particularly aluminium for making Spitfires and Hurricane fighter planes, we would go out, again with the trek cart, and call at houses in the area to see if they had any old pots and pans or other scrap metal which they would give to help the war effort.

Another thing the Scout troop was involved in was acting as casualties or runners when we had any Home Guard or civil defence exercises in our area. We would go to a certain location and have labels attached to us, such as 'broken leg', 'head wound', or 'lacerated arm', etc., and the first aid teams would then practise on us.

Scouts in helmets – there's always someone who has to go one better than everyone else! Notice the national service badge over the right breast-pocket of the Scout, extreme left. (The Scout*)*

Scouts and Cubs collecting wastepaper. The two yellow stripes on the arm of the Cub, fourth from the right, show that he is a sixer, and the colour of the triangle above them shows which six he is in. (The Scout*)*

I am sure our troop was only one of many doing things to help win the war but we all like to think that we made some sort of contribution and 'did our bit'. The Scout Association issued a special National Service badge, worn on the left breast, to Scouts who took part in these various activities.

Geoff Shute:

Just before the war I joined the 24th Ipswich Scout Group as a Sea Scout. There was quite a large contingent of Sea Scouts in Ipswich. An old Thames barge moored on the edge of the channel in the River Orwell, close by Bourne Bridge, Ipswich, was our 'camp' and we could spend weekends on board. It was here that I learned to sail and row. The craft we used were whalers and took a great deal of effort to row as you can well imagine. The Scoutmaster on board was a 'Mousey' Pearce, who ruled us with a plimsoll.

Scouts and Sea Scouts collecting salvage using a handcart. I'm particularly fond of the 'opposition' with their home-made barrow. Notice the boy at the back is still carrying his gas mask in its original cardboard box. (The Scout)

In 1944 a Work Day was organised and Scouts all over England took part in fund-raising activities to finance the Scouts's international relief patrols which followed the Allied armies into Europe, giving assistance to the liberated population.

Over the course of the war a total of 194 Scouts were killed in air raids while on duty.

GIRL GUIDES AND RANGERS

Guides and Rangers helped in hospitals and first aid posts and with the distribution and fitting of children's gas masks. They took part in painting kerbs white and some gave public demonstrations of 'blitz cooking' at the request of the Ministry of Food. Some companies started allotments which the girls took turns to work on. In May 1940 the Guides held a 'Gift Week' during which they raised money by giving up a week's pocket money, or through self-denial, while Rangers and Guiders gave up half a day's pay. Altogether £50,000 was raised for two air ambulances, a lifeboat, rest huts and mobile canteens for the YMCA. The Guides also raised money for the Guide International Service which did similar work to the Scouts's international relief patrols.

Kitty Pledger was a guide in Great Shelford, Cambridgeshire:

Girl Guides group 1945. Second from the left in the back row is Company Leader Kitty Pledger, two along from her is her sister Peggy.

I was a member of the 1st Shelford Guide Company. Besides our Guide work we joined in local fund-raising events to raise money for comforts for the troops. We also collected wastepaper and jam-jars – we were paid a halfpenny for a 1-pound jar and a penny for a 2-pound jar.

These activities were carried out as a company, but we older girls helped at the local military convalescent home. We worked on a rota, two of us going every Sunday morning. We helped with bed-making, cleaning the rooms, serving morning coffee to 'the boys', and with preparing and serving lunch. After we had cleared and tidied the dining room we were given lunch with the staff – we had the same as the boys, which was always a roast dinner, much enjoyed, as with meat rationing we didn't often have a roast at home.

The Guide Association encouraged us by bringing out a War Service badge – this consisted of a gold embroidered crown on a navy-blue background and a separate strip with the year embroidered on it - for each year we did war service we had a new year strip – I did it for two years, 1942 and '43.

Living in the country and not suffering heavy bombing, etc., we were still able to hold our summer camps. We did not travel very far, just to the next village, Stapleford, where we had a very nice meadow with a stream running through it.

Iris Smith was a Guide in Bristol:

I was in the 38th Bristol (Brooklands) Guide Company. When I joined the Rangers, we went over to St Mark's Road where we were trained by the ARP wardens to put out incendiary bombs, they also talked to us about gasses that could be dropped, and what to do if a house caught fire. We also had to be able to cater for 100 people, in case they were bombed out, but luckily I never had to put this into practice. One other thing I remember, we were on a rota, and every Sunday morning, four to six of us went to help at the Bristol Royal Infirmary, cooking and rolling up bandages and the like.

We went on camp once during the war, we stayed in the high walled garden of a large private house just outside Bristol. We went in the morning at 6 o'clock and at 10 o'clock that night we went back to our own houses in case of air raids, then next morning we went back at 6 o'clock, and so on. . . .

Another thing was the Bristol Evening Post used to supply wool, you collected the wool and knitted balaclavas and such for the forces. My mother and I used to do it.

Gwendolen Fox was captain of the 30th Eastbourne (Hamden Park) Guides's Company: 'When war broke out most units closed as the children were evacuated but they drifted back and we had a very good wastepaper collection going. Raising money to send to the Red Cross and various appeals, also keeping the local army canteen supplied with table-tennis balls and buying wool to knit socks, helped by the parents. When I was called up the patrol leaders carried on, helped by one of the elderly Guiders from another unit.'

BOYS'S BRIGADE AND CHURCH LADS'S BRIGADE

The Boys's Brigade provided the ARP messenger service in many places, such as Birmingham. So did the Church Lads's Brigade, as Roy Coles of Bristol remembers:

I was in the Church Lads's Brigade, we mostly did first aid, although the older lads provided messengers for the ARP and the Home Guard and did fire-watching in the evening, not at night. I did it at our headquarters.

I was on the Junior Youth Council which was part of a sub-committee of the local Education Committee. Our purpose was to bring together all the local youth groups, we used to organise parades for things like Warship Week. We also set up a Youth Parliament, and later [after the liberation] tried to arrange a visit to a concentration camp, although sadly this fell through.

AIR TRAINING CORPS AND WOMEN'S JUNIOR AIR CORPS

The Air Training Corps (ATC) was set up in 1941. Its purpose was to give early RAF training to boys aged 16 to 18. Squadrons were set up in schools and universities, or in local areas. Geoff Shute was one of those who joined:

After the war started, and when I was old enough, I joined the Air Training Corps. At the time I was a pupil at the Northgate Grammar School in Ipswich and we had our own Squadron, No. 786. Our evening meetings were held at the school and at weekends we were taught gliding on Ipswich Airfield. There were two other squadrons in Ipswich, No. 188 and No. 262. Needless to say, rivalry between them was intense, especially in the field of aircraft recognition.

A group of about six of us, all members of the ATC, used to spend our weekends cycling to the many airfields surrounding Ipswich. Once at any particular airfield, we would get as close to any aircraft as we could and make notes of serial numbers, camouflage and, in the case of American planes, the squadron and group colours painted on the fins, cowlings, etc.

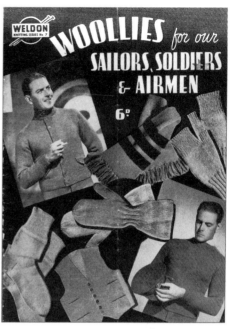

Weldon's knitting pattern, 'Woolies for our soldiers, sailors & airmen'. One way of 'doing your bit' was to knit 'comforts' for servicemen.

Roy Coles of Bristol: 'The school had its own ATC, it was the school's cadet force. We used to go to RAF camps in the school holidays for training. We'd always get to go up in a plane, like a Wellington or an Anson.'

For girls there was the Women's Junior Air Corps, which, like the ATC, was created to give early training for those intending to join the WAAFs. Members were instructed in physical training, games, first aid, morse and similar subjects. Optional subjects included anti-aircraft operational duties, radio location, signals, driving, electrical and engineering work, or clerical and office duties.

AIR RAID PRECAUTIONS

Often, one of the first casualties of a raid was the telephone service, the lines being brought down by explosions. The ARP services needed to send messages to

ARP bicycle messengers, Wallasey; centre is Ken Kessie.

tell the rescue services where people were trapped and so on, and any breakdown in communications would be very serious. For this reason, the ARP services used messengers, who ran messages on foot, or went by bicycle. The messengers were usually young boys or girls. Margaret Ladd lived in Southend-on-Sea:

I think I must have been 16 when I heard that the Civil Defence wanted girls and boys, together with their bikes, to do a messenger service one or two nights a week.

Southend was actually a hive of action during raids, mainly because of being on the River Thames and the soldiers at the artillery garrison at Shoeburyness were trying to shoot German bombers down before they continued up the Thames to bomb London. They hoped that bombs or planes might come down in the river, but a lot of them came down in Southend instead. Of course, there was a lot of shrapnel flying about as well. I remember dodging the hot pieces on the road, hoping that the tyres on my bicycle didn't run over any.

Our activities continued all through the time of the doodlebugs coming over as well. They were OK as long as they kept going but the Ack-Ack fire sometimes caught them over at Shoeburyness and either exploded them or tipped them so that they didn't get to their pre-determined destination. When you heard the engine stop, you hastily looked for somewhere to take cover.

Carol Smith of Dunstable: 'When I was 14 I became a messenger for the ARP because I was used to riding a cycle all over the area. I used to go to ARP classes over an electrics shop in Dunstable, we were taught things like how to distinguish different gasses, also first aid.'

At first, these messengers could be as young as 9 or 10, but soon the minimum age was raised to 16 during the raids, with the younger volunteers being used for post-raid work. Working during a raid could be most dangerous, as this report from 1942 shows:

> Particular praise is given by wardens to several boys who frankly confessed themselves frightened, but still did not hesitate to go out on long and hazardous journeys, not even when flat tyres could have been used as an excuse. Among the messengers was a small, pale boy who begged to be allowed to take a message, but the Chief Warden, feeling that the danger was too great for him, put him off time after time with various excuses, the final one being that he had no bicycle. 'Please, sir,' said the lad eagerly, 'Billy will lend me his bicycle.'

ARP messengers, one a Cub. Soon after the war started, the use of such young helpers was forbidden by the government, concerned about casualties. (The Scout)

After some hesitation the Chief Warden finally sent him off. After a long time, he returned, breathless, wide-eyed and bleeding, and covered with dirt. He asked to speak to the Chief Warden privately. 'Glad to see you back, my boy,' said the Chief Warden as he bent down to listen to the lad's agitated whisper. 'I daren't tell Billy, sir, but I've lost his bloody bicycle. I was blown off it, and when I got up I could only find the front wheel.'

Ken Kessie was from Moreton near Liverpool:

I was 16 when the war broke out. I joined the ARP as a bicycle messenger. I remember one night a piece of shrapnel hit the mudguard and I pulled to a halt, I thought I'd been hit.

Another time a small bomb hit the Rally centre, the ARP headquarters for the village we were in – Moreton. It was a small reconnaissance aircraft that came down in Barnston, it ditched its bombs and one hit the small back room which was used as the messengers's centre. We lost our personal belongings – I lost an air rifle.

And there were other jobs in the ARP. Barbara Daltrey joined the ARP in Windsor just before war broke out. 'I was 16 and a half at the time. I was attached to the first aid parties. My shift was from about 10 pm to 6 am, when I was finished I'd go home for breakfast.' Then there was acting as 'casualties' in training exercises; in *Children of the Blitz*, Robert Westall includes the story of one young ARP messenger who did this: 'There was a label attached to my coat which stated "coal-gas poisoning, not breathing". I lay there for what seemed an age. . . . I was eventually dragged from the ruins and laid on the brick-strewn path whilst being given artificial respiration. My ribs were bruised both front and back. I did not volunteer again!'

In January 1940, as a response to the massive German fire raid on the City of London, Herbert Morrison had brought in the Fire Precautions and Business Premises Order, drafted to ensure that men between the ages of 16 and 60 registered for forty-eight hours's fire-watching a month. Many 16-year-olds were brought into ARP work by this. One such was Bill Sherrington, from South London. *The City That Wouldn't Die*, which chronicles the events of the great London raid of 10/11 May 1941, tells his story:

Down at the Elephant and Castle, incendiaries fell so fast 16-year-old Bill Sherrington dashed to the nearest shelter for help, but found only sour looks –

Boys surveying the remains of their school after a raid. (HMSO)

he must be mad to venture abroad on a night like this. So Sherrington battled heroically on his own, darting into houses the owners had left . . . stamping out some bombs . . . using a stirrup pump on others . . . tipping a flaming flower-box into the street seconds before the window frame caught.

There were many other small local groups. John Merritt remembers one which was set up in Virginia Water, Surrey:

About 1942 I started going to Sunday School at Christ Church in Christ Church Road. At about this time the vicar started a club for its children, boys and girls, and this was to be called the 4Cs club, standing for Christ Church Commando Cadets. This sounds rather military now, and on reflection, it seems to me to have been a mild form of the Hitler Youth. Our uniforms were to have a military look: grey material and a black beret. These never did materialise during my time there – but we did have a badge with 4Cs intertwined on it.

Our activities consisted of map-reading, tracking and signalling, much the same as the Scouts or Guides would have done. I was aged about 9 or 10 at the time and I quite enjoyed our meetings. I think the vicar was the only adult present, as I don't recall any other grown-ups.

NINE

Spare Time

War or no war, for most boys and girls there was still spare time, and children being children they found ways to enjoy themselves.

COMICS AND BOOKS

With no television to watch, no computer games to play, children passed their time in other ways. Comics were immensely popular – there were far more titles available at the start of the war than today. For younger children these included *Rainbow*, *Chick's Own*, *Playbox* and *Tiny Tots*; for older children such favourites as the *Beano* and *Dandy*, *Knockout*, *Chips*, *Comic Cuts*, *Radio Fun* and *Film Fun*. From 1940 paper shortages led to many comics closing down, including *Tiger Tim's Weekly*, *Larks*, *Golden* and *Magic*. No new titles could be started on a weekly basis, but several small publishers produced one-off comics from time to time as paper became available.

Younger children's comics carried on with no change to established contents, but characters in the 'older' comics went to war. *Comic Cuts* had 'Big-hearted Martha, our ARP-Nut', the *Dandy* had 'Addie and Hermie', alias Adolf Hitler and Herman Goering, shown as inept food thieves, while the *Beano* featured 'Musso the Wop', alias Mussolini. Barbara Courtney: 'We used to read comics, the *Beano* and the *Dandy*, my favourites were Desperate Dan with his great big steaks, and Lord Snooty.' Iris Smith: 'I used to get half a crown [2s 6d; 12½p] a week pocket money. I bought the *Girl's Crystal* comic every week – we used to take it down into our shelter – we had an Anderson – and Mrs Brain – she and her husband lived with us then – used to read the serial *Barry and his Mobike* to us all.' – unlike many of today's comics, there would be several written stories in a comic of the time, so they lasted for hours.

As the war progressed those comics that remained got smaller; before the war many had been the size of newspapers. The number of pages also decreased; in 1939,

Cover of the Beano *comic, July 1941. With Hitler is Herman Goering, the head of the German Air Force. The hidden propaganda message is that, while rationing was bad in Britain, it was even worse in Germany – 'half a sausage between us'. (© D.C. Thompson & Co.)*

for example, the *Beano* usually had twenty-eight pages, by 1940 it was down to eight, with colour printing used only on the cover.

The US forces brought with them glossy American comics such as *Superman* and *Batman*. These seemed even more glamorous compared with their monochrome wartime British cousins. Charles Harris: 'I never got pocket money – I used to earn 6*d* going out with the baker on his round. We spent it mostly on sweets and comics, the *Beano*, the *Dandy*, the *Rover* and the *Hotspur* were my favourites. We also got American comics, like *Superman*, and *Batman*, but they were thick, like books. When you'd finished with them we used to swap.'

Most comics produced a Christmas annual, and this continued throughout the war. At the beginning of the war other books were produced with the war in mind, such as the *Black-out Book*, designed to be used in the shelters: 'Here is the ideal companion for those black-out evenings – a volume which has been aptly described as "The One Hundred and One Black-Out Nights's Entertainment". Problems which Father will enjoy solving, quiet corners for Mother, puzzles and things to make for the children, games and competitions, nonsense rhymes and brain tests for the entire family' – it almost makes an air raid sound fun!

Children's books also continued to be produced, some using the war as a background for their adventures. Richmal Crompton's hero William Brown had a wonderful chance to exercise his 'talents', in *William and the ARP* (1939) later published as *William's Bad Resolution, William and the Evacuees* (1940) later published as *William the Film Star, William Does His Bit* (1941), *William Carries On* (1942), and *William and the Brains Trust* (1945). Among other things, William manages to have fun helping refugees, in air-raid shelters, collecting salvage and chasing suspected spies, hoarders and black marketeers, as well as causing trouble for an air-raid warden, the Auxiliary Fire Service and, of course, the police.

Enid Blyton continued to produce children's books throughout the war, although the war itself was rarely mentioned in them. Her output was prolific, with over 100 titles published between 1939 and 1945. Some were for smaller children, such as *Five O'Clock Tales* (1941) and *Enid Blyton's Happy Story Book* (1942). For older girls, she produced, among others, the St Clare's series of books, the first, *The Twins at St Clare's*, appearing in 1941, followed through to *The Fifth Formers of St Clare's* (1945); St Clare's was a girls's boarding school which the war seems to have passed completely by. For boys and girls the Famous Five appeared in *Five on a Treasure Island* (1942), *Five Go Adventuring Again* (1943), *Five Run Away Together* (1944) and *Five Go to Smugglers' Top* (1945).

Funny Comics: this is one of many wartime comics produced from time to time as paper became available.

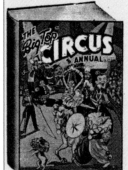

Two Jolly Gift-Books for Boys and Girls

EVERY child loves the Circus— and they will love The "Big Top" CIRCUS ANNUAL, too! This new 168-page book will thrill boys and girls of all ages. There are 32 pages in colour, showing Circus Acts, and dozens of exciting stories—all well illustrated. This is the perfect gift for every child who loves animals and circuses.

The "BIG TOP" CIRCUS Annual

Price 5/-

OVER 120 pages of microphone mirth! Flanagan and Allen, Sandy Powell, Revnell and West, Tommy Trinder, "Big-hearted Arthur" and all—lucky children with this Annual will find them, with lots more of their radio favourites in sparkling fun in RADIO FUN ANNUAL. This is a grand book of mirth in picture and story.

RADIO FUN ANNUAL

Price 2/6

On Sale at all Newsagents and Booksellers.

'Two jolly gift books for boys and girls' advertisement from Woman and Beauty magazine, November 1939; Radio Fun was a particular favourite.

W.E. Johns's hero, Biggles, once again took to the air – although he would by now have been well into his forties, having become a fighter ace in the First World War – in eleven wartime books, spanning almost every corner of the war. Titles included *Biggles Secret Agent* (1940), *Biggles Defies the Swastika* (1941), *Biggles Sweeps the Desert* (1942) and *Biggles in Borneo* (1943).

In 1941, Johns introduced a new female character, Worrals, in *Worrals of the WAAF*. She went on to appear in *Worrals Flies Again* (1942), *Worrals Carries On* (1942), *Worrals on the Warpath* (1943), *Worrals Goes East* (1944) and *Worrals of the Islands* (1945).

Malcolm Saville began writing at this time, publishing his first book *Mystery at Witchend* in 1943, followed by *Seven White Gates* (1944), *Trouble at Townsend* (1945) and *The Gay Dolphin Adventure* (1945), which has lost, or perhaps gained, something in the changing use of language over the years.

RADIO

The BBC had been broadcasting television programmes since August 1932, but television sets were available only to the rich – for the vast majority of people the radio, or the wireless as it was called, was the main form of home entertainment. It was on the wireless that most people heard the Prime Minister announce that Britain was at war. Television broadcasts ceased immediately, and the radio schedules were changed – a new version of the *Radio Times* was even rushed out on Monday 4 September with the new schedules in. The children's programmes were broadcast in *Children's Hour*, between 5 and 6 o'clock, every day but Sunday. The original choice for that Monday, the first day of the war, was scheduled as:

Another story of Samuel the Snail
Some favourite gramophone records
The cases of Constable Crush
The best and easiest way to keep fish

There is a saying that truth is the first casualty of war. On Wednesday 6 September children's programmes were back, but only for *half* an hour, and so they remained throughout the war – they were still called *Children's Hour*, so in that sense the *Radio Times* was, in a way, correct, but the children were not fooled. However, this was partly made up for by the fact that an edition of *Children's Hour* was introduced on Sundays.

Up to 18 September 1939, the *Radio Times* published no details of what was on *Children's Hour*, but from that date the programmes were listed again, starting with *Another story from Mostly Mary*, followed by *The Zoo man*.

The programmes continued to be introduced by 'Uncle Mac' (Derek McCulloch) with the words, 'Hello children everywhere', and besides short programmes of the sort already mentioned, there were serialisations of classics, such as

Rupert and the banjo—33

In another moment other boards are pushed aside and a strong young man comes in and joins Rupert and stares at him curiously. "How on earth you came aboard I don't know," he smiles, "but you've done me a very good turn. You must explain later. Now I must force this door. I hate breaking up my own ship, but I must get at those two young buccaneers without delay."
ALL RIGHTS RESERVED.

NEW RUPERT BOOK

The war will not deprive children of one great joy they look forward to at this time of the year—Rupert's Adventure Book. It is on sale today, better than ever, and **printed for the first time in full colour.**

There was never another Rupert Book like it for the happiness that is packed between its covers, and for the beauty of its multi-coloured pictures of Rupert, Bill Badger and Podgy Pig. It contains eight long, complete stories and over 400 illustrations.

Rupert's new Adventure Book (published only by the Daily Express) is on sale today, price 3s., at all newsagents and bookstalls, and the Daily Express Offices in Fleet-street, E.C.4. By post for 3s. 7d.

Rupert continued to appear daily in the Express *throughout the war. Here in September 1940 there is also an advert for the Rupert book, 'in full colour'. (© Express Newspaper Group)*

THREE SWASTIKA PUZZLES

A. NEW DEAL FOR NAZIS

With 12 playing cards form a square as illustrated.
Now, take 4 more playing cards and form a swastika inside the square frame.

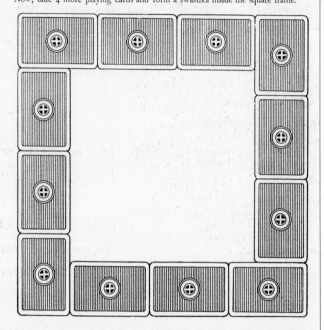

B. GETTING SQUARE WITH HITLER

Trace this swastika on paper, or draw a new one. It is easy to draw because it is made up of 17 perfect squares.

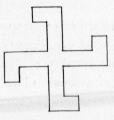

Now for the puzzle. Cut the swastika into four pieces which can be put together to form a perfect square.

C. HITLER'S FAVOURITE CARD GAME

Take four playing cards. Place them so that they form a swastika.

Three Swastika puzzles from the Brighter Blackout Book, *published in 1939; solutions can be found at the back of* A Child's War.

Toad was just passing underneath the bridge when . . . !

In the next episode of Kenneth Grahame's story 'The Wind in the Willows', this afternoon at 5.0, you will hear of plots —and counterplots.

Radio Times *illustration for* The Wind in the Willows.

The Wind in the Willows, and *Great Expectations*, and old favourites such as *Toytown*, with 'Larry the Lamb'.

Sylvie Stevenson: 'We used to listen to *Children's Hour* on the radio – there was Uncle Mac and *Toytown* – I liked that. Then there were the serials. We also listened to the Ovaltinis on Radio Luxembourg.'

During the day there were two sessions of broadcasts for schools, 11.00 to 12.20 and 1.50 to 3.00. A typical programme might be:

11.00 Announcements and singing
11.05 British history – from coast to coast
11.25 Singing
11.30 Interlude
11.35 Nature study
11.50 Physical training

Radio Times *illustration for a Tommy Handley show. Tommy Handley's show* ITMA *was one of the war's great favourites.*

The schools programmes proved to be especially useful to those pupils who had not been evacuated and had no schools to go to, or to those receiving home tuition or part-time schooling.

Of course children listened to other programmes too. Particularly popular were *The Brains Trust*, a discussion show; *Paul Temple* and *Appointment with Fear* – thrillers; *ITMA* ('It's That Man Again') a comedy hosted by Tommy Hanley, which included such characters as Colonel Chinstrap, Mrs Mop and Funf; and another favourite, *Charley McCarthy*, a ventriloquist act (Charley was the dummy!).

Popular singers included Vera Lynn – the 'Forces's Sweetheart', Arthur Askey, George Formby, Hutch – real name Leslie Hutchinson, and Gracie Fields. There were also bands such as Geraldo's Orchestra. Live bands always featured at local dances (discos not yet having been invented). Ken Kessie recalls one in Moreton:

You had the hops, the dances on Saturday night, you met your girlfriends there. The music was played by 'Alberto and his Band'; a saxophone, a drum kit and a piano. Alberto, he was never really Alberto, probably Albert, he played the saxophone.

THE CINEMA

In the absence of television, the cinema was one of the most popular forms of entertainment – almost everyone went to 'the pictures', at least once a week. Iris Smith: 'Every Saturday we queued up for the cinema – there were long queues – everyone went to the pictures – my favourite was Judy Garland.'

In addition to the feature film, which was the main entertainment of the evening, there would be a second or 'B' film, one or two cartoons – such as Disney's *The Fuhrer's Face*, where Donald Duck dreams he lives in Nazi Germany – and the newsreel. Ken Kessie: 'My favourite was Betty Grable – the flea-pit in

Moreton was a must on Friday or Saturday, Sunday it was closed of course. We all went to church on Sunday morning – mostly to see the girls.'

No film programme of the time would have been complete without a ten-minute newsreel, made by Pathé Gazette, British Movietone News, Gaumont British News, British Paramount News, or the American 'March of Time' – in the absence of television these were the only moving pictures of the war the British public saw. There were usually also Ministry of Information films, such as *Five Inches of Water*, which showed why it was important to use only a small amount of water in the bath, or cartoons such as *Dustbin Parade*, showing the importance of salvage collecting – all done with a certain amount of humour.

Wartime films can be split into two types. First there were those based on the war, telling stories, usually adventures, in which the heroes fight Nazi spies, etc. Among these was the 1942 classic *Went the Day Well?*, in which the inhabitants of an English village, including a young evacuee played by Harry Fowler, fight off Nazi storm troopers. Second there were what we might call 'escapist' films, such as Disney's *Dumbo*, released in 1941, which had nothing to do with the war, but which helped people to forget such things as the Blitz – but only for a while. Charles Harris:

Then, of course there was the pictures, we used to go Saturday morning. If you went to the cinema in the evenings, when there were the air raids, if there was an air-raid warning, they used to put up a notice on the screen saying 'The sirens have gone if you want to go to the shelter', but they kept on showing the film, we always stayed to watch the end.

Particular British favourites included George Formby, top British box office star from 1939 to 1943 – Formby always played the same character, an amiable idiot who always won through in the end. His wartime films included *Let George Do It* (1940), where he took on Nazi spies; one scene, in which he dreamed of flying to Germany in a balloon and punching Hitler on the nose, was a huge success, British audiences cheering at the top of their voices. In another film, *Get Cracking* (1943), George played a Home Guard. Other comedy favourites included Arthur Askey, and the Crazy Gang, a comedy group which included Bud Flanagan, who years later sang the theme tune to the BBC's comedy series about the Home Guard, *Dad's Army*. Of course, they were not universally popular – Charles Harris recalls: 'I couldn't stand Arthur Askey, "big-hearted Arthur" they used to call him, we called him "big-headed Arthur"!'

International stars popular in Britain included Abbott and Costello, Bob Hope, Jimmy Cagney, and those perennial children's favourites, Laurel and Hardy who continued to make films throughout the war, including *Air Raid Wardens* in 1943.

The war took its toll on the stars as well as everyone else. In June 1943, Leslie Howard, the second biggest British box office draw at the time, was killed while travelling in an aeroplane that was shot down over the Bay of Biscay; rumours at the time said that the Germans thought that Churchill was on board. Also thought to have been shot down was the American band leader Glenn Miller, whose aircraft went missing on 15 December 1944.

SPORT

Then, as now, many children followed sport keenly, having their favourite teams and players. In the 1930s football and cricket players had regularly starred in cigarette card sets, and in the first weeks of the war the newspapers featured star players who had joined the armed services or civil defence. The radio and cinema newsreels covered matches, as well as the newspapers, and many children continued to attend local fixtures.

As soon as war broke out, the government, worried about air raids, banned all events that attracted large crowds. This, of course, included football, rugby and cricket matches. The newspapers announced: 'All sport brought to a halt'. However, the government soon realised that sports fixtures helped to boost morale and a limited programme of such events was introduced. Of course the black-out meant that there could be no floodlit night-time events; this particularly affected greyhound-racing and speedway motorcycle racing, a sport which had been a pre-war favourite. Large indoor events were also affected as stadiums were taken over for use as ambulance or fire stations, or converted to factories. Even Wimbledon was not exempt: the courts were spared from being used for vegetable growing, but the car park was turned into a farm and the buildings used as an ARP centre.

In football, representatives of the Football League and the Football Association at first decided that all league and cup matches would be suspended. By the middle of September friendlies were being played, but the size of crowds was limited to 15,000 in even the biggest grounds. By now it had become impossible to resume the pre-war competitions; many players had joined the armed forces or civil defence, and fuel shortages meant that team travelling had to be cut back. From the end of October, a regional competition was set up comprising eight groups;

French Army *v.* British Army

At 3.45 a commentary will be broadcast on the second of the three football matches between the two armies. The matches are being played in different military centres to allow as many troops as possible to see the games. A commentary on the first match was broadcast last Sunday and the third match will be described on February 18.

Radio Times *illustration for a football match between the British and French army XIs. Such fixtures replaced the pre-war internationals.*

South A, made up of London teams, South B, South Western, Western, Midlands, East Midlands, North Western and North Eastern. There was also a series of international matches played between the home countries and our allies.

The FA cup was not played for throughout the war, leaving Portsmouth, who had won it in 1939, holding it until Derby County took it in the 1946 final, but in March 1940 a 'War Cup' competition was introduced. Following a knockout format, it took just seven weeks to produce its first finalists, West Ham and Blackburn Rovers, with West Ham winning 1–0 at Wembley. By now the 'phoney war' was over; among those watching the match were soldiers, admitted free, who just one week before had been taken off the beaches at Dunkirk. The crowds differed from those before the war, not only in size and in the preponderance of uniforms, but because that standard accessory of the pre-war supporter, the football rattle, was banned – it was too much like the gas warning!

Professional football continued to be played throughout the war, although the standard was often poor due to the lack of available players; there were also many local matches, often fund-raisers for 'Warship Week', or the 'Spitfire Fund'. Usually played between police, fire brigade, civil defence or service teams, they often featured celebrity players.

Cricket was badly hit. The normal three- or five-day matches were no longer possible, and the cricketing authorities, old-fashioned as ever, seemed unable to imagine anything else. Gradually cricket evolved into a series of one-off, one-day games, with new scratch teams springing up – the two most successful being the grandly named British Empire XI, and the London Counties XI.

BOMB-SITE PLAYGROUNDS

When all else failed, there were always the bomb sites to play in. The gutted shells of houses made perfect adventure playgrounds, as we might call them today. In the worst-hit areas these bomb sites could cover extremely large areas, as is shown in the post-war films *Hue and Cry* and *Passport to Pimlico*. Barbara Courtney remembers playing on bomb sites: 'We used the loose bricks to lay out room shapes, and then we built chairs and tables and swept the rooms clean.' Slowly the bomb sites began to blossom as the wild flowers took root there, especially the rose bay willow herb, which was nicknamed 'Bombsite' by London's East Enders.

Kids playing amidst devastation – bomb sites made great playgrounds.

TOYS

At first British toy manufacturers responded to the war by producing a whole range of military toys: tanks, aircraft, ships, soldiers, even barrage balloons. There were several high-quality German toy manufacturers before the war such as Schuco and Bing, but British companies were only too happy to fill the void. Particular favourites were board games and card games, which could be played in the shelter, or during the black-out. However, as the war drew on, raw materials became scarce, and the toy factories were turned over to war production. Like everything else, toys were in short supply. People made their own, or repaired old ones. Charles Harris: 'I got hold of a big old wooden train, I painted it blue and put a seat on it and gave it to my little brother.' Many fire stations set up workshops where staff in off-duty periods would build or renovate toys for local hospitals, etc.

The *Lewisham Borough News* in December 1941 reported:

CHRISTMAS TOYS FROM SALVAGE WASTE 'The finest collection of toys I have seen this Christmas' remarked the Mayor of Lewisham at a children's party given by the Wardens of Forest Hill. Out of material salvaged from bombed houses the Rescue Service members had made all sorts of attractive toys, which, in view of the shortage in the shops, were particularly appreciated by the 54 children who had been invited to the party. There were toy engines, train sets, dolls's cots, rocking horses, bead frames, and other toys. The gifts were distributed by Father Christmas (Rescue Party Leader Mills).

GETTING UP TO NO GOOD

Too much spare time with the schools closed, too little to do, and an absence of parental control could have negative effects – juvenile crime, or juvenile delinquency as it came to be known, was a particular problem of the war. In *It Came to Our Door*, his book about Plymouth during the war, H.P. Twyford explains the problem:

DECEMBER 9, 1939

Keep the Children Happy with MICKEY'S FUN FAIR

GROWN-UPS WILL LOVE IT, TOO! MAKE SURE YOU HAVE A PACK OF THIS NEW WALT DISNEY CARD GAME FOR CHRISTMAS!

Draw the curtains, forget your cares and enjoy a game of MICKEY'S FUN FAIR! You'll find that the children adore it, and before you know what's happening, you'll be enjoying it as much as they!

Donald Duck, Goofy, Snow White, Horace Horsecollar and lots more of Walt Disney's clever characters are featured. This is a game of tense excitement and laughter—just the tonic to chase the blues away.

Pepys Series

Every good stationer and store sells "Mickey's Fun Fair." Published by Castell Bros., Ltd., London and Glasgow, by permission of Walt Disney-Mickey Mouse, Ltd.

88 CARDS IN FULL COLOURS

Mickey's FUN FAIR CARD GAME

Endless Entertainment

Value Unequalled! No Increase in Price

FUN FOR ALL WITH DISNEYS

2/6 PER PACK

The first Christmas of the war was very little different to those before it. Toys and games such as this were easy to come by.

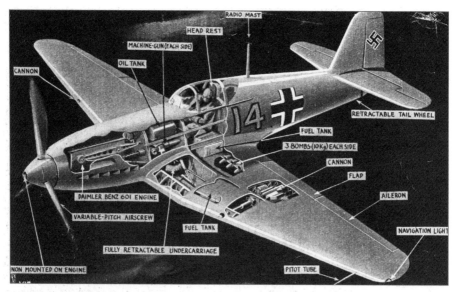

Illustration of a German Heinkel 113 from the War Illustrated *magazine of August 1940. Such pictures of enemy and Allied aircraft were very popular with children.*

There was, of course, an increase in crime, although I do not think anyone would be justified in saying that it was a serious or alarming increase. I think the greater concern was in the matter of juvenile crime. Many children seemed to be lacking in the old-time home discipline. This was perhaps understandable to some extent, because so much former parental control was missing by reason of fathers being away in the Services and mothers often engaged all day on war work.

It was by no means only a problem in Plymouth. The war record of the Metropolitan Police states: 'Children neglected or getting into mischief – or worse – through the absence of parents, were abnormally numerous.' In *Raiders Overhead*, Barbara Nixon, an air-raid warden in London's East End, gives one example of some of this 'mischief':

In one shelter where we cleared a bay of its bunks to make a recreation room, the children themselves helped with the clearance, carefully counted the nuts and bolts, and behaved in an exemplary fashion. The next night, their games became distinctly noisy, and some women protested with vigour. The children retaliated by pouring water down the ventilation pipes onto the bunks below;

A toy factory in August 1940; notice the war toys, tanks, barrage balloons, etc.

the women, thereupon, made use of two broomsticks, and the children capped that by resorting to the iron bunk poles. Peace was, with difficulty, finally restored, but the next morning the children had the final word. They threw all the precious nuts and bolts through the windows of the houses. And the ringleader of it all was a chubby little person called Pozzie, who would always proudly announce that he was 'eleven, rising twelve'.

Ken Kessie remembers high spirits in Moreton: 'The Presbyterian Minister started a youth club, but we wrecked the place – we were as bad as the youths today really, although there was no violence.'

A certain amount of actual crime was, of course, carried out by youths, but most of it was of a fairly petty nature, usually perpetrated by boys between 16 and 18. The biggest area of crime (60 per cent) was 'larceny and housebreaking', followed by 'theft from parents or employers' (11 per cent). This extract from the *Kentish Mercury* is fairly typical: 'James Kemp (17) and a 16-year-old youth pleaded guilty to stealing from a shop articles valued at £4 10s. The younger boy's parents were dead, and both lads had been sleeping in air-raid shelters.'

Model German and British aircraft; soon after this photograph was taken, toy factories were turned over to war work.

In June 1941 the Home Office and the Board of Education jointly issued a memorandum on juvenile crime. They pointed out that the number of children under 14 found guilty of offences in the first year of the war had risen by 41 per cent, and for the fourteen to seventeen year old group the increase was 21 per cent. It was felt that a major cause of these increases, besides lack of discipline, was the closure of leisure facilities due to the war; as a result of this, in London, play centres were opened in all areas, and staff were sent to the reception areas to organise out-of-school activities. For older children 'mixed youth recreation centres' were opened, for young people to 'meet in social intercourse and recreation'.

TEN

High Days and Holidays

If Britain was going to be invaded, the invaders would obviously land somewhere on the coast, almost certainly in the south or east. Almost from the start of the war beaches in these areas were planted with mines, barbed wire and other obstacles, so swimming, paddling or playing on the sands there were out of the question. From time to time areas of Britain, especially along the coast, were closed to visitors; in April 1944, for instance, all civilians (except those who lived there) were banned from a coastal belt, 10 miles in depth, stretching from the Wash to Land's End.

Family holidays became a rarity as workers were no longer given holiday time – war production had to be kept to a maximum. Added to this were the travelling restrictions – 'Is your journey really necessary?' the slogan asked. Petrol for private cars was almost impossible to get, and anyway most of them had had their tyres removed for the rubber salvage drives, and railways were needed for the transport of troops and war materials. What transport was left for civilians was often in a poor state. Charles Harris: 'Most of the buses were so old that when they went up Chingford Mount they couldn't get all the way up with passengers on board, they'd stop half way up, then we'd all get off and walk up to the top and then get back on.'

There was *some* travelling, though. Special cheap-day and weekend excursions were laid on by bus and railway companies, for parents who wished to visit their evacuated children. But on the whole, holidays stopped. If you lived in a blitzed city, you might be lucky enough to have relatives

One of the most famous posters of the war, 'Is your journey really necessary?' Transport was needed for war materials and troops. (HMSO)

in a country area who would put you up for a week. Other than that, holidays tended to be for children only, organised by clubs, or groups such as the Guides. R.J. Holley of Bristol remembers one camp:

During the war we went as schoolchildren to summer camps helping the farmers bring in the harvest, etc. We, that is, Eagle House Youth Club under the direction of the Rev. Bouquet, the club leader, went to the Duke of Beaufort's estate. He had a miners's camp there. During the war the duke let it to the schoolchildren and clubs who went to help on the land.

Eric Chisnall:

An incident I well remember concerned a week's holiday with our Scout troop. A new vicar came to the church and he took over as our Scoutmaster. He was not over-popular with us lads as he tried to stop our rather boisterous games such as British Bulldog, because he thought they were too rough. He very kindly arranged for several of us to spend this holiday in Rugby, in the parish he had served in before coming to Ipswich. As I had never travelled more than fifteen miles from home, this was a great adventure, and it was probably the same for most of my mates.

In Rugby people were very kind and we were made very welcome even though we did have to sleep on a hard wooden floor in a local hall. Amongst other trips we were taken to see the famous Rugby School and the Rugby railway locomotive engineering shops, and a trip to Coventry was also arranged.

When we arrived our vicar gave us a stern lecture about not being too extravagant with food, as people had kindly given up their rations to feed us. At breakfast the next morning he proceeded to smother his toast with a thick layer of butter, and what looked to me like well over a quarter of an inch of marmalade. He thought he was sparing, but coming from a family of eight children, well used to 'scraping it on and scraping it off again', I could not believe my eyes – at home we were rationed by price as well as by ration coupons.

Incidentally we ate most of our midday meals, we did not call it lunch in those days, at the British Restaurant in the town centre.

Carol Smith:

One year twenty of us from the Girls's Club went with Miss Brown to North Wales for our summer holiday. It took us 24 hours by train because of wartime hold-ups at Crewe. When we arrived at Bangor it was Sunday, we were unable to get any food to eat, everything was closed in Wales, so as there were no buses running either, we had to walk 12 miles to Snowdonia Youth Hostel.

The following year about the same number of us went to Derbyshire for a YHA walking holiday.

In 1942, the Government introduced the 'Stay-at-Home Holiday Scheme'. Under this industrial workers were given a week's leave 'for recuperation' but were encouraged to spend it at home. Local entertainment and recreation were the order of the day, and to this end local councils and organisations laid on such things as fêtes, concert parties and bands.

The maxim 'Eat, drink and be merry – for tomorrow we die' was very much the case for many in the Second World War. Barbara Courtney from Nunhead fondly remembers the parties they had: 'We used to have parties at the weekend all the time – people brought whatever food they could get – drink too, they

Deptford children's concert in aid of National Savings, August 1943. (Lewisham Local Studies Library)

Standard indoor fireworks advertisement, 1939. Soon all gunpowder production would be solely for the war effort.

'Knitted cuddlies' from Gifts You Can Make Yourself.

got somehow – we often had them at my Nan's – we were just glad to still be alive.' All over the country, especially at Christmas, children's parties were organised by the ARP, the police, or other local services.

There was one high point most families could look forward to. George Parks remembers his older brother coming home on leave:

> When Harry came home we always had a party; relatives and neighbours would come round, not so much his friends, they were all in the forces too. I used to go around with him when he let me – he'd be in his uniform and the other kids were so jealous. This was only a few times though; they didn't get that much leave.

Celebration of Guy Fawkes Night disappeared during the war. Fireworks were impossible to come by – all gunpowder production was obviously reserved for the war effort – and even had they been available, letting off fireworks or burning bonfires at night were both banned as part of the black-out regulations. Besides, for many people the sights and sounds of a fireworks display were far too like those of an air raid to be seen as enjoyable at the time. Fireworks, like street-lights, took on the mantle of the fruits of peace – things to look forward to once the war was over.

FOOD FACTS
CHRISTMAS FANCIES'

Of course you can't find Christmas fancies as you could before the war, but there are some you can make for yourself. Gingerbread men and paper-wrapped toffees will help to fill the children's stockings, and the Christmas cake will look twice as festive with a coating of icing.

GINGERBREAD MEN

Ingredients : 2 oz. sugar or syrup, 2 oz. margarine, 8 oz. plain flour, ½ level teaspoon mixed spice, 2 level teaspoons ginger, lemon substitute, 1 level teaspoon bicarbonate soda. *Method :* Melt in a pan the syrup or sugar and margarine. Pour into a bowl. Add some flour and the spice and lemon substitute. Stir well. Dissolve the bicarbonate of soda in a tablespoon of tepid water and add to the mixture. Continue stirring gradually adding more flour. Finish the process by turning out the mixture on to a well-floured board. Knead in the remainder of the flour. Roll a small ball for the head, flatten it and place it on the baking tin. Roll an oblong for the body and strips for arms and legs. Join these together with a little reconstituted egg and put currants for the eyes.

HONEYCOMB TOFFEE

Ingredients : 2 oz. sugar—demerara if possible, 4 oz. syrup, 2 level teaspoons bicarbonate of soda. *Method :* Boil syrup and sugar together for about 5 minutes, or until it is a rich brown colour. While still boiling stir the bicarbonate of soda in very quickly. Pour into a well-greased sandwich tin, and allow to cool and set. When almost firm, loosen edges with knife and turn out on to wire tray.

ICING *made with ordinary Sugar and Household Milk*

Ingredients : 4 level dessertspoons sugar, 6 level tablespoons Household Milk, dry, 2 tablespoons water, colouring and flavouring. *Method :* Mix sugar and milk together. Add water and beat till smooth. Add colouring and flavouring and spread on top of cake.

LISTEN TO THE KITCHEN FRONT ON TUESDAY, WEDNESDAY, THURSDAY AND FRIDAY at 8.15 a.m.

THE MINISTRY OF FOOD, LONDON, W.I.   FOOD FACTS No. 233

Christmas Food Facts – the Ministry of Food produced many of these food facts adverts; this is number 233.

The first Christmas of the war was almost the same as those of the pre-war era, but as time wore on and shortages began to bite, wartime Christmases became ever more 'makeshift' affairs. Toys were hard to find in the shops, decorations and trees were scarce, so once again it was time to 'make do and mend'. Sylvie Stevenson recalls Christmas in wartime Chingford: 'I remember watching my dad working on these things in the shed. Then at Christmas all the kids got these ducks he'd made, you put them on a slope and they waddled down it.' Barbara Courtney: 'At Christmas we used to make all our own decorations, we cut them out of cardboard and sweet papers, stars, elephants, all sorts of shapes, Chinese lanterns as well. Dad always managed to get a tree somehow. If you didn't have a fairy, you used a small doll, or cut out a star.'

And food rationing, even though the government increased the rations over the holiday, meant the usual feast had to be cut back. The Ministry of Food and the writers of other wartime recipe books did their best to find substitutes, with varying degrees of success, as these Christmas recipes demonstrate:

A Wartime Christmas Pudding (Food Facts for the Kitchen Front)

This pudding was made in Canada during the last war [the First World War].

Mix together 1 cupful flour, 1 cupful breadcrumbs, half a cupful suet, half a cupful mixed dried fruit, and if you like a teaspoonful of mixed sweet spice. Then add a cupful of grated raw potato, a cupful of grated raw carrot, and finally a level teaspoonful of bicarbonate of soda dissolved in two teaspoonfuls of hot water. Mix all together, turn into a well-greased pudding bowl. The bowl should not be more than two-thirds full. Boil or steam for at least 2 hours.

Emergency Cream (1942) (Ministry of Food)

Bring a half-pint of water to blood heat, melt a tablespoonful unsalted margarine in it. Sprinkle 3 heaped tablespoonfuls household milk powder into this, beat well, then whisk thoroughly. Add 1 teaspoonful sugar and 1 teaspoonful vanilla. Leave to get cold.

Christmas Fruit Pies (1942) (Ministry of Food)

This mixture is a good alternative to mincemeat.

Warm 1 teaspoonful marmalade (or jam, but this is not so spicy) in small saucepan over tiny heat. Add a quarter-pound of prunes (soaked 24 hours, stoned, chopped) or other dried fruit, 1 tablespoonful sugar, 1 teacupful stale cake crumbs, or half cake, half bread crumbs, half a teaspoonful mixed spice. Stir together until crumbs are quite moist. Remove from heat, add 1 large chopped apple; also some chopped nuts if you have any. Make up into small pies, or large open flans. The mixture keeps several days in a cool place.

Christmas Cake with Holly Leaf Icing (1945) (Ministry of Food)

THE CAKE 4 ounces sugar, 4 ounces margarine, 1 tablespoonful syrup, 8 ounces flour, 2 level teaspoons baking powder, 1 level teaspoon cinnamon, 1 level teaspoon mixed spice, 2–4 eggs (reconstituted), 1 pound mixed fruit, half a teaspoonful lemon substitute, pinch of salt, milk to mix (about one-eighth of a pint).

Cream sugar and margarine, add syrup. Mix flour, baking powder, salt and spices together. Add alternately with the egg to the creamed mixture and beat well. Add fruit and lemon substitute and enough milk to make a fairly soft dough. Line a 7-inch tin with greased paper, put in the mixture, and bake in a moderate oven for 2 hours.

HOLLY LEAF ICING For this you will need: 4 ounces soya flour, 2 ounces margarine, 2 ounces sugar, 4 tablespoons water, almond essence to taste, few drops of green and red cookery colouring.

Melt margarine and water together, stir in the sugar, then the essence. Divide about a quarter of the resulting liquid into two cups, a little more in one than the other, and keep warm. Stir about three-quarters of the soya flour into the bulk of the liquid, turn out, knead the paste thoroughly, pat to about one-eighth inch thick, press on

Holly-berry set from Gifts You Can Make Yourself *– shortages of goods in the shops meant that people often made presents themselves, and there were many books and pamphlets produced to help them.*

Ration-book case from Gifts You Can Make Yourself.

top of cake and neaten edges. Put a drop or two green colouring into cup holding most liquid, stir in flour and treat as for plain paste. Cut into leaf shapes, mark veins with a knife, pinch round edges to form 'prickles'. Put red colouring into other cup, treat as before, form red paste into tiny balls. Arrange leaves and berries on top of cake in wreath shape or sprays, as you fancy.

ELEVEN

Peace

Germany surrendered on 7 May 1945, and the next day was declared VE (Victory in Europe) Day. Up and down the country street parties were organised, although the food shortage meant that the food was somewhat restricted. Many people have vivid childhood memories of this time.

Charles Harris: 'On VE Day we had a party, we held it in the Reliance Garage because it was pouring with rain. Every house gave what they could, jellies and things, junket. I won a packet of tea!'

Derek Dimond: 'On VE Day they set up a street party in the road outside the Dog and Duck – I remember we had jelly, which was a real treat. On VE Night they set up searchlights in the Square in Stanstead and people danced in the street. I remember watching the moths fly into the searchlights.'

Sylvie Stevenson: 'I shall never forget VE Day – we went over the fields to the shelters. We said "We won't need these any more". They had a corrugated iron escape hatch, we were all jumping on and off. I caught my leg on the edge – it cut me to the bone – I've still got the scar.'

David George from South Ealing clearly remembers VE Day: 'They had a street party down the corner from where we lived, they brought out all the Morrison shelters and made one long table with them. People knew the end was coming and had been saving up their rations – for the first time in ages we had toffee – suddenly there was uproar, one girl was in floods of tears – her mother and father took her home – she'd pulled out a tooth on one of the toffees.'

Japan fought on, but after the Allies dropped atomic bombs, first on Hiroshima, then on Nagasaki, they also surrendered and 15 August was pronounced VJ (Victory against Japan) Day. The Second World War was finally over. Christine Pilgrim from Peckham clearly recalls her feelings: 'VJ Day – what a relief it was – I know it sounds cruel now, but those atom bombs falling – everyone cheered, they just wanted to finish it off. The jubilation was huge.'

R.J. Holley: 'I was at the Duke of Beaufort's estate, for VJ Night, and the Duke had a barbecue, cooking a deer on a spit.'

The war was over and the fathers who had gone to serve were coming home, although not always to the welcome they were expecting from their children. Elizabeth Brown from Walthamstow remembers her husband's homecoming:

My husband, Len, had joined up in 1939, and my second child, Carole, was born in 1942, after he'd been on leave. When Len came home, late in 1945, Carole didn't know him, and when he first came in she ran and got behind the door – to her he was a stranger. She was so jealous – she'd had me all to herself before – if he was going out and came over to kiss me goodbye, she'd come and push herself between us. She was also jealous of her older sister, Patsy. Patsy was born in 1936, so she remembered Dad – she was all over him, and this made Carole worse. It took Carole ages to get used to him. My Mum lived

A wonderful handmade VE Day outfit.

Testing the street lights, 1945. After six years of black-out the sight of street lights proves fascinating to these children, the youngest of whom would never have seen them on before. (Lewisham Local Studies Library)

VE Day street party. (Kent Messenger Newspaper Group)

two doors away, so if Carole saw Dad coming home, she used to go to Mum's –
luckily Len understood.

Also coming home were the evacuees. Some found their houses gone, others
that their families had abandoned them or refused to have them back, but for
most it was wonderful. Christine Pilgrim went home to Peckham: 'We came
home again in May, at the end. I was so thrilled, it was like belonging again. We'd
been in Bournemouth, at a sort of children's hostel called "House Beautiful", the
staff weren't very beautiful – they didn't like the children much, and we didn't
like them. You should have heard the rudeness that came out when we knew we
were going home!'

The war certainly affected every British child, but in different ways. For a few,
it was a great adventure, for others, a waking nightmare, but for most it was a
mixed experience. In *William Carries On* published in 1942, Richmal Crompton
gives some of the pros and cons of a wartime (country) childhood:

Certainly the war seemed to have altered life considerably for William.
Sometimes he thought that the advantages and disadvantages cancelled each
other out and sometimes he wasn't sure. . . . Gamekeepers had been called up

and he could trespass in fields and woods with impunity, but, on the other hand, sweets were scarce and cream buns unprocurable. Discipline was relaxed – at school as the result of a gradual infiltration of women teachers, and at home because his father worked overtime at the office and his mother was 'managing' without a cook – but these advantages were offset by a lack of entertainment in general. There were no parties, summer holidays were out of the question because of something called the Income Tax, and for the same reason pocket money, inadequate at the best of times, had faded almost to vanishing point.

Vivien Hatton: 'I was moved around so much during the war that I finished up with a lack of confidence and a great deal of insecurity. It was all so frightening.'

Barbara Courtney: 'Of course you hated the war just because it *was* a war, but you did have great friendships because of all the sharing.'

Christine Pilgrim: 'I hated the war – I couldn't watch any of the 50th anniversary VE Day celebrations – I hated it all so much – just little things like you never knew whose dad was going to be killed next.'

Sylvie Stevenson remembers the war with a child's practical eye: 'I was only 4 when the war started so I didn't really know any different – it wasn't particularly enjoyable,

Children's fancy dress competition. (Lewisham Local Studies Library)

VE Day street party, Chingford. Sylvie Stevenson is peering out behind the last girl seated on the right. Notice the Union Jacks on the houses.

there was too much destruction. Later on, when I was about 12, I looked back and thought, "I missed so many things – especially ice cream."'

The war was at an end: evacuees and troops were returning home, the black-out was over, air-raids and V weapons a thing of the past. Yet some problems lingered on: shortages got worse and rationing was to remain until 1953, while bomb sites continued to be a feature of the landscape of many towns into the 1960s. Now little is left, street shelter signs are a rarity, ephemera and artefacts are keenly collected, but what does endure are the memories of those who were there.

It had been a war that had affected civilians as never before, and children perhaps most of all. In Germany the last defenders of the Reich had been the old men of the Volksturm and the boys of the Hitler Youth. Millions of British children had been evacuated, their education had been disrupted, their family life turned upside down by the absence of fathers, and even mothers. For a great number of them nightmares and nervous problems would haunt them for years. In so many ways, it had truly been a child's war.

8th June, 1946

To-DAY, AS WE CELEBRATE VICTORY, I send this personal message to you and all other boys and girls at school. For you have shared in the hardships and dangers of a total war and you have shared no less in the triumph of the Allied Nations.

I know you will always feel proud to belong to a country which was capable of such supreme effort; proud, too, of parents and elder brothers and sisters who by their courage, endurance and enterprise brought victory. May these qualities be yours as you grow up and join in the common effort to establish among the nations of the world unity and peace.

George R.I.

Certificate given to all schoolchildren in June 1946 as part of the first anniversary celebrations of the end of the war.

Bibliography

August, Evelyn. *The Black-out Book*, Harrap, 1939

Blake, Lewis. *Red Alert*, Lewis Blake, 1982

Chase, Joanna. *Sew and Save*, Literary Press, 1942

Collier, Richard. *The City That Wouldn't Die*, Collins, 1959

Craig, Elizabeth. *Cooking in Wartime*, Literary Press, 1942

Crompton, Richmal. *William and the Evacuees*, Newnes, 1940

——. *William Carries On*, Newnes, 1942

Food Facts for the Kitchen Front, Collins, 1941

Front Line, HMSO, 1941

Gifts You Can Make Yourself, Odhams Press, 1944

King, Muriel. *Let's Play Firemen*, Raphael Tuck, 1943

Knitting for All, Odhams Press, 1941

McCarthy, Tony. *War Games*, Queen Anne Press, 1989

'Make Do and Mend', Ministry of Information, 1943

Nixon, Barbara. *Raiders Overhead*, Lindsay Drummond, 1943

Page, Hilary. *Toys in Wartime*, Allen & Unwin, 1942

Practical Family Knitting Illustrated, Odhams Press, 1944

Rag-Bag Toys, Dryad Press, 1942

St George Saunders, Hilary. *The Left Handshake*, Collins, 1948

The Schools in Wartime, Ministry of Information, 1941

Thomas, Howard. *The Brighter Blackout Book*, Allen & Unwin, 1939

Twyford, H.P. *It Came to our Door*, Underhill, 1945

We Think You Ought to Go, Greater London Record Office, 1995

Westall, Robert. *Children of the Blitz*, Macmillan, 1985

LEAFLETS

Civil Defence leaflets
Dig for Victory leaflets
Grow More Food – pub. Ministry of Agriculture & Fisheries, 1939
Ministry of Information leaflets
Potato Pete's Recipe Book – pub. Ministry of Food, 1945
Red Cross leaflets

PERIODICALS, 1939–45

Beano
Dandy
Kentish Mercury
Lewisham Borough News
Picture Post Magazine
Radio Times
Woman & Home Magazine

Index

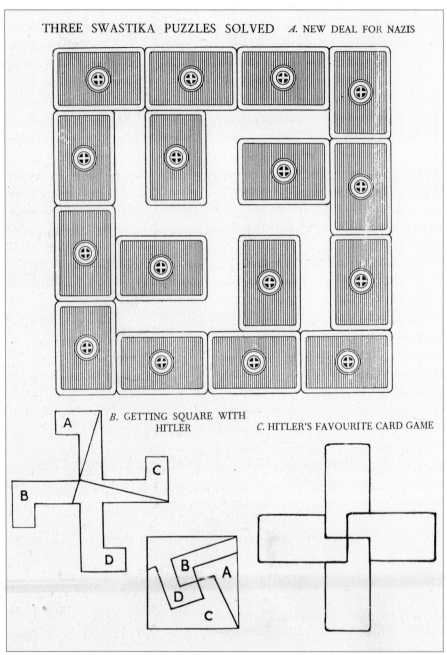

THREE SWASTIKA PUZZLES SOLVED   *A.* NEW DEAL FOR NAZIS

B. GETTING SQUARE WITH HITLER

C. HITLER'S FAVOURITE CARD GAME

Solutions to the Swastika puzzles from The Brighter Blackout Book *reproduced on p. 90.*